REFLECTIONS

OF

SUNFLOWERS

REFLECTIONS

OF

SUNFLOWERS

RUTH SILVESTRE

Allison & Busby Limited
13 Charlotte Mews
London, W1T 4EJ
www.allisonandbusby.com

A CIP catalogue record for this book is available from
the British Library.

First published in Great Britain in 2004
by Allison & Busby Ltd (ISBN 978-07490-8345-8).
Reissued in 2010.

10 9 8 7 6 5 4 3 2 1

ISBN 978-0-7490-0848-2

Typeset in 11/15.5 pt Sabon by
Allison & Busby Ltd.

The paper used for this Allison & Busby publication
has been produced from trees that have been legally sourced
from well-managed and credibly certified forests.

Printed and bound in Great Britain by
CPI Bookmarque Ltd, Croydon, Surrey

RUTH SILVESTRE is a singer and actress, her most famous role being Dulcinea in *Man of La Mancha* at the Piccadilly Theatre. She has published many articles on France, and a number of children's books. She divides her time between London and France.

Available from
ALLISON & BUSBY

A House in the Sunflowers
A Harvest of Sunflowers
Reflections of Sunflowers

For Mike

CHAPTER ONE

Our past twenty-four summers have been spent at Bel-Air, our second home in south-west France, with a brief, gardening visit in early spring. 'Well, that's a first!' I remember a bright young woman completing a survey at Gatwick saying, when we gave 'To cut the grass' as our reason for flying that April. This year however, a year in which we had expected to celebrate our quarter of a century in this lovely corner of France, brought unforeseen challenges.

In January my husband Mike was diagnosed with colon cancer. Fortunately, an operation was swiftly organised but our usual spring visit was, of course, impossible. The grass did not get cut. Would we even see our garden that summer? It seemed unlikely. In the frightening realities of a crowded hospital even our London home became, for me, just a place in which to sleep between long, anxious hours by his bedside. Our other home in France seemed a far-away fantasy. Bel-Air stayed shuttered and silent.

At long last, the news was better. A summer visit became a possibility. We both longed to go. For me the waiting was especially hard as I spent two days in June recording my first book, *A House in the Sunflowers,* for Isis Talking Books, and the memories of all our early adventures were re-awakened. By July, Mike's next hospital appointment was not for six months. We finally booked our tickets and kind friends opened and cleaned the house for our late arrival in mid-July. And there in the sunshine, the quiet and the sweet, clean air, we began the road to recovery.

Driving all the way not being an option, we put the car on the train to Brive, by far the easiest way to do the journey – providing you do not get lost in Calais between the tunnel exit and the motor-rail terminal. After having done just that, I realised on checking the map with the written instructions that they did not agree. *Nul point le navigateur,* stick to the map next time. After an inevitable, tedious wait for the cars to be loaded we found our minute but comfortable cabin and while other travellers unpacked champagne and prepared to celebrate, we thankfully settled ourselves on the firm beds and slept for eight hours. Ingenious manoeuvres were necessary to wash and dress, but there was good coffee and fresh bread waiting in the station buffet before the sheer exhilaration of heading south.

It is a heavenly drive through the valley of the Dordogne in the very early morning. At Beynac we stopped for a drink. Not yet nine o'clock, the first day-trippers were just arriving. In the nearby hotel, guests lingered contentedly over *petit déjeuner*. Like a cohort of black-clad space warriors, intrepid elderly cyclists in trendy helmets descended, red-faced, from the steep road to the chateau. They huddled briefly to check their maps before speeding away. The Dordogne, ageless and indolent, willows reflected in her dark water, advertised boat trips to see '*Les Quatre châteaux*' and I enjoyed my first *jus d'abricot,* a drink inexplicably absent in bars in England.

We were reluctant to leave without at least going to see the magnificent chateau of Beynac a little closer, but it turned out to be even further up the steep road than we thought. When we turned the last curve and reached the top, the ancient *bourg* was silent and the castle towered above it, enormous and imposing. How powerful those medieval lords must have felt surveying their terrain from such a viewpoint. We postponed a real visit for another year and slowly wound our way home through the Dordogne and into Lot-et-Garonne.

We always call first at the large farmhouse on the edge of the village, where *les Bertrands,* Raymond and

Claudette, our farmer friends live. We bought our house from them originally, they farm all the land around us and, over the years, have become like family. Claudette was picking strawberries. She stood up, waved and came to greet us with the bowl, almost full, under her arm. Raymond appeared from the barn and he and Mike wept as they embraced. We had made it after all.

As we drank outside in their flowered courtyard I noticed my large hydrangea, which normally stands in its pot by my porch, now here, sheltered by an overhanging shrub and covered in blooms. It had never looked so beautiful.

'It was easier to bring it down, *en pension* with the others than go up to Bel-Air to water it,' explained Claudette. My geraniums, my elephant's ear and my great hibiscus, which my cousin David bought me as a small plant years ago, always descend to the shelter of farm when we leave at the end of September. Claudette has a specially constructed shelter where she over-winters her wonderful collection of plants. Chilean begonias, tibouchina, plumbago, bougainvillaea, and a huge lemon tree, all wait there for the last frosts to pass. It is prudent to wait. Not for nothing are Saint Mammert, Saint Pancrace and Saint Servais, all unfamiliar to me, called les *Saints de glace,* the ice saints. Their feast days fall in late May, and frosts as late as this are not unknown and can be disastrous in this region of plum orchards. These days safely past, and the sun grown stronger, all Claudette's tender shrubs are moved out into the courtyard to join the clematis, the oleanders and whatever new plants she has chosen for that season.

'I've already taken up some of the small pots and put you in a few petunias,' she said. 'The key is in the door. It all looks very spick and span. She's certainly worked hard, Susan. *Même pas une toile d'araignée!'* she giggled. 'There's not even a cobweb.' The spiders round here are the fastest workers I know.

When, so long ago, we first set eyes on Bel-Air, our quaint little house, it had been empty for many years. The rough, stone walls were almost invisible behind tall, straggling, box trees and long neglected vines and creepers. Inside the air was thick with dust, one wall stained with a trail of green lichen and the well worn, old furniture shrouded in cobwebs so thick that one was sure that Sleeping Beauty herself must be nearby. A bat skimmed out from under rotting floor-boards, and looking up through the broken tiles one could see the sky. It certainly bore no resemblance to the kind of properties one now sees on those endless TV programmes where hopefuls search for their dream home in the sun. No designer kitchen here, no luxurious bathroom, no lavatory or even running water; just a well with a broken pump – and yet we were so sure that it had been waiting just for us.

–◇–

Now, the morning sunlight glinted on the long slope of the repaired roof. The pots of petunias that Claudette had planted flashed their bold colours from the low walls we had built in front of the porch. Even the brass door-knocker that I had bought in a junk market had been polished, a rare event. The windows gleamed. Inside it was just as Claudette had said, and, as usual, she had put flowers on the long table and a bottle of wine. But it was so extra especially clean. We marvelled as we went from room to room. We knew how much hard work had gone into this transformation by Susan, encouraged by her mother, our old friend Ursula. Ursula, grandmother of thirteen and great grandmother of twenty-three at the last count, had arrived to see us many years ago on her horse because she'd read the first book about Bel-Air. Susan can turn her hand to anything and has her mother's style and energy. She had left our house sparkling.

But even if the spiders had not had time to draw breath, other creatures had already invaded. As I switched on the light in the pristine bathroom I saw two baby mice asleep in the bath, curled round each other. Woken by the light they made frantic but useless attempts to climb out. Tiny round bodies, large ears and long snouts, it was unthinkable to kill them, especially in the bath. With difficulty we scooped them with the back brush into a carrier bag and transported them a long way away down the track, urging them not to return. Where they came from and how they got into the bath remains a mystery. They certainly were not there when Susan left barely an hour before we arrived.

If you live in a house as ancient as ours with small gaps between old window-frames and under old doors you get accustomed to visitors from the rolling countryside which surrounds us. We take for granted the praying mantis on the draining board, the sight of the pale underbelly of a tree frog, its fingers splayed on the window-pane, the lizard basking on the sill, the toad in the dustpan. Mice are a nuisance, but usually leave when we turn up. Other creatures sometimes pose more of a problem.

One year we arrived to inspect our newly tiled porch. We had in fact waited a long time for it to be completed. The previous year we had chosen the terracotta tiles. They matched the interior, but were specially fired to withstand frost. Daniel, the tiler, the son-in-law of the ex-Mayor, was young and enthusiastic

'I will just continue the line from inside the door,' he said. 'It will be *impeccable.*' The boxes of tiles stood ready. He dumped a load of sand in front of the porch, stuck his shovel in the top and whizzed off again to get the cement. When he did not re-appear that day or even the day after, we shrugged, disappointed but imagining that, like many busy workmen, he was doing two jobs at the same time. It was Raymond who told us that on his way back to us Daniel had collided with an out of control Mercedes and his injuries were so severe that he would probably never work again. Worrying about our porch seemed inappropriate, the pile of sand and the shovel at its jaunty angle a painful reminder.

The following spring we contacted the tiler from Villereal, about ten kilometres away. M. Carnejac had, in fact, done the floor in our main living room many years before and, much later, our bathroom. He quite understood why this time we had engaged the tiler from our own commune.

'*C'est normal,*' he said when he came up to see us. Yes, he would have it ready by the summer. *Pas de problème.*

The old porch had once been cemented and cut with grooves, presumably to resemble large tiles, but it still looked just like cement and the dust and rubbish, which collected in the grooves, was maddeningly difficult to clean.

Now, our newly tiled porch was as splendid as we had hoped and only needed sloshing down with a bucket of water. But we had, it seemed, a mystery visitor. Each morning we would notice a small puddle on the outside edge of the porch. What could it be? Jean-Michel, Raymond's son-in-law, up to look at the cows, gave us his opinion. 'Oh, *ce n'est qu'une chatte sauvage,*' he said. 'She is marking her territory.'

We had often had wild cats in the barn, and many spitting little offspring. This marking of territory was new. I was not convinced. Mike, who is not a cat lover, constructed a fragile device with sticks and a battered old tin on top. 'That will give her a fright,' he muttered.

When the sticks were still in place the next morning but splattered with liquid we were both perplexed.

The following day I was reading in a chair facing the porch when I suddenly heard the sound of splashing. Down from the roof came a stream, falling in exactly the same spot. Now I knew the reason for the occasional scrabbling we had thought we might have imagined in the rafters. It was not mice, or even a rat. It was the dreaded *fouine,* the stone marten. They have been known to chew through all the electric wiring and roof insulation in the houses of friends and they are devilishly difficult to trap. And she had the cheek to have chosen to site her latrine right over our new porch!

As usual it was to Raymond that we turned for advice. He unearthed a cage, which he sometimes used to set to catch coypu, the scourge of nearby ponds and lakes. It was both large and heavy, not a problem when one slides it along a bank through the tunnels of grass which the coypu, known locally as *le ragondin,* makes; much more difficult, however, to hoist it up a ladder to the attic. Raymond wore gloves as he carefully unwrapped an egg for bait from his handkerchief.

'She has a formidable nose,' he whispered, 'but she can't resist an egg.'

He set the egg in the centre of the trap, carefully avoiding moving the base, which pivots, sending both ends crashing down to trap the animal without wounding it.

'What will you do with it if we catch it?' I asked.

'*Il faut la tuer,*' he answered. I must kill it.

Two nights later, just as the sun slid down, I saw *la fouine* silhouetted against the darkening sky, racing along the whole length of the ridge of the roof. She didn't take the egg but she took the hint and moved house. So far she has not returned.

After the removal of the mice and the inspection of our unusually impeccable house, we backed the car up to the porch and began, slowly, to unload, first the contents of the cold box into the fridge. As our journey had been unusually rapid, we had brought a large piece of smoked gammon, which Raymond and Claudette had first tasted and pronounced delicious when they had once come to stay with us in London. We normally take three or even four days driving down through France, exploring as we go, and any gifts we bring them must inevitably be well-preserved. This would be a treat. It is so difficult to begin to repay the delicious surprises that Claudette has over the years prepared for us; the *écrevisses* flambéed in Armagnac, her own guinea fowl cooked with tiny *champignons,* the rich *civet de lièvre,* and all her improvised miracles, savoury rice pudding with courgettes, chicory wrapped in *crêpes* in béchamel, not forgetting the famous *tourtière,* the gigantic *baba au rhum*...She is a splendid cook.

At last the car was cleared, we moved it out of sight round the corner and, our final task, we made the bed. Sitting outside again, we spent a long time just gazing at the view. There was nothing to do now until eight o'clock when, as always on our first evening, we would go down to the farm to eat and catch up on the news. We drifted about in the garden, wading through the long grass, bright with wild flowers. What was that we'd planted over there? We couldn't even remember. We had had so many other things to worry about. It seemed an age since we had last come. How long would it take us to get all this wilderness into some shape? Had we even the energy? What did it matter? We were here.

We would, after all, spend this special summer in our beloved house. We had much to be thankful for.

CHAPTER TWO

The gammon wouldn't keep forever and on Sunday it was Raymond's birthday. As I didn't feel quite up to preparing the whole meal I did what everyone does locally and ordered a very large *tarte aux fruits.* I knew it would look splendid and taste delicious.

'Quelques prunes et poires?' queried the pale faced *boulanger,* his eyebrows powdered with flour. *'Quelques framboises aussi, peut-être?'*

'Perfect. Anything but strawberries,' I said. I knew that Claudette had an abundance this year.

I also dispensed with making soup as the last few days had been extremely hot, and decided to construct a large dish of hors-d'oeuvre from *macédoine* of vegetables and tinned crab in a lemon mayonnaise, surrounded by hard-boiled eggs, avocado, and sweet, field tomatoes. I par-boiled the gammon the night before and stripped off the skin.

Next morning, after collecting the tart, imagining myself well ahead of schedule, I lingered at a local gardening market. A mistake! And, in any case, buying plants for my wilderness of a garden was not so much foolishness as complete delusion. I looked at my watch and fled to buy a tin of diced vegetables on my way home to augment the fresh ones already prepared.

FERMATURE EXCEPTIONELLE said the notice on the village shop. *Exceptionelle* it most certainly was and very inconvenient. It meant a trip into Monflanquin, our nearest town, on a Sunday morning early in the season when *tous les vacanciers* would be stocking up. It was just as I feared. The supermarket was packed. There was nothing to be done but wait patiently in the queue and amuse myself, comparing the clothes and the contents of the trolleys of the French, the Dutch, the English and the occasional American. It was almost midday by the time I returned to finish my preparations *a toute vitesse*.

We would be eight. Sylvie was the first to arrive, having come furthest, from Villeneuve-sur-Lot. We first met when I was searching in the archives there where she then worked. As together, on a rainy morning, we had pored over an ancient map we had discovered that Mike and I had bought the very house where her great-grandfather, Celestin, had been born and had lived until he married. From his daughter, Sylvie's grandmother, I heard more about her aunt, Anaïs, my predecessor at Bel-Air. I learnt that she came in 1889 as a bride of eighteen, to marry Celestin's brother, Justin. How they had one son who was handicapped as a result of an illness, probably polio, and that after Justin died in 1918, mother and son lived at Bel-Air until Anaïs died aged 92. I learnt how hard she worked and how she loved her garden. The roses, the iris, and the lilies which sadly always flower just before we arrive, were all planted by her, long ago. Small wonder that, when I first saw Bel-Air, even in its derelict state, I felt a sense of those seventy-four years of caring.

Fortunately, all my other guests were late. The strict rules about *midi-et-demi* for lunch have been gradually eroded by the next generation. When the old people were alive they were always on time. Véronique, Raymond's daughter, and her husband Jean-Michel strolled up from their house on the other side of the orchard, their daughter Océane, now eight, still drying her bright pink nails. She is not much younger than her mother was when we first came. A plump shy ten-year-old, who helped us sweep out the cobwebs and gave me dictation to improve my French, Véronique is now extremely svelte and the deputy mayor.

Raymond came to apologise for Claudette who had still not returned from her second '*vide-grenier*' of the morning. The local version of a car boot sale,

Claudette can't resist them. They are so popular now that there is one somewhere almost every weekend. Of course the real bargains are to be found when a whole village turns out its attics for the very first time. Then you must be up really early to beat the dealers. With their sharp and expert eyes they soon scoop up great grandmother's old soup plates, copper preserving pans or her heavy, folded, linen nightdresses. You might find the proverbial dozen, damask, dinner napkins, long forgotten, with hand-embroidered initials, or pillow-cases trimmed with handmade lace. There are photograph albums, old lamps and tarnished silver. Claudette is still searching for an old bread slicer but she usually finds something to amuse her. After an aperitif Raymond went back to the farm to fetch her and this time, with many a blast on the klaxon, they drove up in the newly refurbished 1929 Citroen. It now looks very different from the time we first saw it over twenty years ago.

Matthew, my younger son, and Raymond's Philippe were much the same age and in those early days while Mike and I worked on the house they spent a great deal of time roaming about together. Phillipe's English was better than Matthew's French but they both benefited. One day Philippe took his new English friend to see his Grandpa's car. Matthew came home in great excitement.

'It's brilliant!' he said. 'It's really old. You should see it. It's huge. And you know what? It's even got DUNLOP written in English on the spare wheel.'

Raymond owned a barn close by the church, which he never seemed to use. We had presumed that it was simply inconvenient, being a distance from the house. We had no idea that inside the rough stone walls was a museum. When the following day Raymond and Grandpa pushed open the massive doors we saw that the vast space was crammed with ox carts and traps and antique farm implements. We stood in amazement while the boys scrambled to the back where we could just glimpse the Citroen up on blocks and protected by old blankets and sacks.

'Can we uncover her now, Papi?' begged Philippe.

The old man nodded and we stood round admiringly as she was revealed in all her stately glory. Grandpa brushed the high, dusty mudguard with his small gnarled hand and told us that she had been there ever since the war. They had successfully hidden her from the Germans who were then commandeering every vehicle. He patted her bonnet and smiled. He seemed perfectly happy to leave her there for another forty years but everyone else was eager to bring her out and, a few days later, with most of the village as spectators, she was ceremoniously towed from the barn and trundled off to be repaired. Claudette's cousin, the mechanic in a nearby village, was delighted when he eventually made her roadworthy and drove her back in triumph to the farm.

Not surprisingly her progress could be erratic. Over the years, mostly on Sunday afternoons, Mike and Raymond, accompanied by anyone intrepid enough to withstand the noise, the draught, and the occasional breakdown, have made sporadic trips to surrounding villages. Recently, however, Raymond decided that it was time to have the Citroën completely refurbished. Now the dark green bodywork gleams, the nickel sparkles, and she has beautiful new leather upholstery which is much more comfortable. Indicators are the only addition. Just as, all those years ago, the car conferred status and glamour on Granny and Grandpa—he was the only young man anywhere in the region with a car she once told me, smiling—now it does the same for Raymond. He has a new identity as a proud member of the *Club des Anciennes Voitures de Villeneuve*. They plan many trips, prudently always complete with a mechanic and spares.

The meal was a success. The gammon appreciated, although I almost ruined it at the last moment by putting it under the grill to caramelise the sugar on the crisscrossed fat, studded with mustard and cloves. I am still not used to cooking with electricity and can't believe how long it takes to heat the oven. The grill, however, is quicker. The gammon was rescued just in time. As we were drinking our coffee Philippe and Corinne, his wife, arrived with eleven-year-old Clement. They were looking very fetching in twenties costume and straw boaters and had come to borrow the old Citroën to complete the effect and to visit friends. Clement presented his grandpa with a rose for his birthday and the young family drove off sitting up high and waving regally from the very smart, old car. Raymond had to leave, too, as the wheat was ready and the *moissonneuse* due that afternoon. He is part of a farmers' cooperative who must wait their turn for the combine. Naturally everyone needs it at the same time and there are many anxious moments and frantic phonecalls when the crop is ripe and rain is threatened.

All our guests gone, we dozed in the shade wondering when M. Escoffier would arrive to open the pool. We had already been here three days, three very hot days, and the sight of the heavy, mudstained, blue winter cover still securely in place was extremely frustrating. Once upon a time we would have just got on with it ourselves but those days are, sadly, over. We knew, of course that M. Escoffier, like the combine, was simply overloaded with work.

We had first met him the previous summer. He had a stand at the local fête. We had only just arrived and for some reason had been quite unable to contact our ebullient M. Bourrière who always dealt with our pool, or his manic son.

It was most unusual. We had written to fix a rendezvous, as we always did, before leaving England. They had given us excellent service for many years, ever since the day when they arrived with the digger and the first great clods of earth were gouged out of our meadow. It took us so many years to decide to have a pool, both for aesthetic and financial reasons, but we have never regretted it.

Until now, it was always a confident, red-faced, M. Bourrière in his cowboy boots who would arrive promptly to solve any problems. He replaced our calcified filter when, one summer, the chalk level in the water was too high, and he changed the location of our pump. The original underground plastic pump housing, with its large heavy lid, had two disadvantages. It was not frost-proof and therefore the pump had to be removed for the winter and replaced in the spring, and in the summer, the shelter and dark humidity proved irresistible to snakes.

For many years at Bel-Air we never saw a snake. I was actually quite miffed when others told of the size of the one they had seen in their garden. They are not vipers, just harmless grass snakes, called here *couleuvres,* but they can be two meters long and have thick bodies. Mike does not care for them but I wanted to see one at close quarters. Our mayor, now retired, told me a tale of once being summoned in a hurry by the holiday-makers from Colchester who were staying in his *gîte* next door.

'*La dame a crié, "snick! snick!"*' he told me dramatically. '*C'était un grand serpent.*'

He killed the snake and gave it to his somewhat eccentric English neighbour who said she would like to show it to her children. The following day she invited the mayor, his wife and his tenants to dinner. One of the courses was a delicate slice of something in a good sauce. After they had all eaten and pronounced it delicious she revealed that it was in fact '*la couleuvre*'. The mayor laughed, showing his gold fillings, as he described the horrified reaction of les *Anglais de Colchestaire*.

'*Mais ce n'était pas mal du tout,*' he said musingly.

Mike became very tired of our resident snake. He carried a large stick to thump on the lid before lifting it to check the filter. Eventually he had had enough. M. Bourrière and his son removed the pump from underground and promised to build us a *cabine*. It would solve the problem of the snake, they said, and also the over-wintering of the pump. We imagined a sort of small sentry box but arrived back one evening to find a substantial Wendy house complete with window.

But where was M. Bourrière the next summer? It was a mystery. He didn't even answer the phone. M.

Escoffier, standing calmly behind his stand at the fête with samples of plastic pool liners and pictures of other pools, simply smiled and shrugged. He is the complete opposite of M.Bourrière, being dark, slender and very quietly spoken. He must have known that his competitor had gone bankrupt and disappeared, but he said nothing. He was presumably aware that, eventually, we would inevitably be in touch.

About eight-thirty in the evening we saw with relief his white van snaking up the track.

'Trop de travail,' he said clambering wearily out. 'Et comme toujours – tout au même moment.'

We watched with pleasure the heavy cover being rolled back and saw that the water was clear above the muddy bottom. Tomorrow we would swim. We left him quietly and methodically going about his work, almost in the dark by now, and went down to the farm at about nine-thirty for, as we thought, dessert and champagne and to give Raymond his birthday present, which we had forgotten to do earlier.

They had only just begun their meal. At the long table under the hangar, where we have eaten so many alfresco meals, sat the whole family with both the grandchildren. There was also the driver of the combine, his hair full of chaff, the amiable patron of the farmers' cooperative and Ken Farrington, our nearest English neighbour who had let his house and was consequently homeless that night and staying with Raymond and Claudette. We resisted the soup, the home-cured ham and melon, the galantine of chicken; but the roast veal...It smelt so good...

'*Servez-vous, Servez-vous,*' called Claudette.

'*Eh, oh, il faut manger, Michel,*' urged Raymond. 'You need to build yourself up.'

Well, perhaps. Just a taste. Plates and cutlery appeared like conjuring tricks. We gave in. The moon appeared round the edge of the roof. Much, much later a large cake was carried in, candles were lit, Raymond opened the champagne and we all sang '*Bon Anniversaire*'.

Chapter Three

And the next day we swam. We thought it might be prudent to wait for the water to warm up but by 11.30 the sky was a blazing blue, and the stones on the terrace burnt our feet. The water was only 20 degrees but, oh, the joy of plunging in for our first swim of the holiday. Actually, a holiday was not the most accurate description of the next few weeks as we wrestled with the garden, falling asleep, exhausted, every time we sat down, ten minutes turning mysteriously into half an hour.

The worst battle was with the pampas grass, which should, of course, be cut back in December. As we are never here in the winter and as it looks too glorious to cut when we leave in early October, it is always a sorry sight by the following spring. It was an even sorrier sight by July. Our long hedge of pampas protects the pool from the east and the forty to fifty silvery plumes are reflected in the blue water when the sun is low. They *are* beautiful, we always tell ourselves, as with long sleeves, long trousers and strong gloves to protect our wrists, we struggle to twist out the old stalks and cut the hedge back without ruining the newest shoots.

When we began to trundle the debris down to the rubbish heap we found we had another problem. At the end of the previous summer we had been unable to have a really good bonfire. The maize harvest was unusually late and with our bonfire site close to Raymond's field there was a risk of setting the whole crop alight.

'We'll leave it till we come in the spring,' we had said. But of course fate had intervened and we had not come. And now the great sodden pile was still there and a new crop of maize, already head high, rustled gently in the heat. It looked as though, by the end of the summer, our heap of garden rubbish would be larger than the house.

As a change from gardening we slowly began to carry out all the outdoor furniture, most of it stored in the north-facing bedroom. As it is the one used by my two grandsons it is the least tidy, but as we gradually unearthed piles of chairs and tables we were unable to find two umbrellas and two recliners. We looked in the other rooms. Where on earth had we put them?

They were not to be found. Perhaps Raymond and Claudette had borrowed them. It seemed unlikely but we do frequently borrow from each other. Or perhaps Véronique and Jean-Michel had needed them for a party?

After lunch we wandered down through the lower wood, across the stream and up through the meadow, to Raymond's farm. Those cows still in the barn lowed as they heard us approach, the young hunting dogs barked furiously, racing frantically up and down inside their compound, but there was no one else at the house. They were all away. Raymond and Claudette, as we later learnt, on a motoring spree in the old Citroen and the others at the coast. There was no sign of our chairs and umbrellas. We walked back, skirting along the edge of the field to where Jean-Michel had recently finished building a splendid terrace by their new pool, and it was clear that they had ample furniture around it without ours. We climbed slowly back up again, crossing through the orchard, grateful, this time, for the shade from the plum trees already heavy with fruit. As we reached the top of the rise and glimpsed the roof of our new Wendy house we began to laugh. Of course, that's where we had put them. We'd simply forgotten. Our preoccupations of the past worrying months had eroded so many memories, or perhaps we were just having a 'senior moment' as a friend calls her forgetfulness.

As we cut the grass we found other forgotten delights, a white, double althea, planted the previous summer, the fat buds almost ready to open. There were strong new shoots on a hardy hibiscus, which has spectacular pink flowers as large as a tea-plate, and a row of montbretia glinted through the grass. But the gardening debris was piling up and, after a few days, we were simply too weary to move it. There were sprawling heaps all over the place. At just the perfect moment, two strong young men arrived, Mike's godson, Guy, and his friend, both just down from university. They were very keen to earn some Euros, they said, as they downed a cold beer, and promised to solve all our problems the following week.

On Saturday we took a day off. We went to market at Villeneuve-sur-Lot, an elegant small town, which somehow manages to preserve much of its medieval past while flaunting many stylish boutiques and bars. Outside the old Porte de Paris, one of the original thirteenth-century gateways, the wide boulevard is built where once the moat, for hundreds of years, helped to defend the town. A raised flowerbed now colours its entire length, beneath lagerstroemia trees pink with blossom. There are hanging baskets and tubs on every corner dripping with petunias, bidens, and whatever else is in horticultural vogue that season.

Set back, further down the boulevard, is Villeneuve's controversial new town hall; the old, fine building near the river having become too small to contain the ever-burgeoning bureaucracy that is the curse of France – and of everywhere else, come to think of it. It is a bold attempt to blend the old and the flamboyantly modern. Opinions vary as to its success. Presumably they could not entirely demolish the sixteenth century convent which, gracefully if shabbily, spanned the far end of a simple, bare square with a few benches for weary shoppers. Here, *pétanque* was played under the trees and on the second Tuesday in the month the stalls of *la Friperie,* the flourishing second-hand clothes market, unfurled their ragged line of bright umbrellas all down one side of the square.

Today each classical end-wing of the convent remains but the entire centre of the old building has been demolished and replaced with a startling 21st-century statement of municipal pride. The changes to the rest of the square are easier on the eye. It is laid out as a formal garden where you may sit and marvel at the impeccably weeded and watered lawns and flowerbeds. The planting is stunning. There are beautiful swathes of colour, and many unusual varieties. *La Friperie* would, of course, completely spoil the image, and has been banished. We must now take our tape measures to the farthest and least elegant end of the boulevard if we wish to browse through the crumpled garments and find a bargain.

Villeneuve really was new in 1263. It is one of a

chain of small, fortified towns, or *'bastides'*, created across the south-west of France by Comte Alphonse de Poitiers, brother of King Louis. In the middle of the thirteenth century he came south to inspect his new territories of Quercy and Agenais, which he had acquired by his marriage to Jeanne de Toulouse. He found a region devastated by the wars between the church and the heretics of the time, the Cathars. Their beliefs were named in France *l'Hérésie Albigeoise,* being most powerful around the town of Albi. The people of the south-west were to pay heavily for their religious defiance. Marauding northern knights, sanctified by a church alarmed by the fervour of this growing heresy, rode south on a crusading opportunity conveniently much nearer home than the Holy Land. They did not discriminate. Anyone who spoke the *langue d'Oc,* the language of the south, was deemed to be a heretic. The whole region was pillaged and the massacres were ferocious.

No doubt Alphonse, as he travelled in the aftermath of such destruction, soon realised that there would be little revenue to be collected from such an impoverished region. To become prosperous again it needed completely replanning. Near to the Benedictine Abbey of Eysses he saw what could be a fertile valley. *'Un endroit suffisamment spacieux et convenable,'* as it was then described in the charter which was drawn up. The nearby Château of Pujols on the hill had been completely destroyed, but, he reasoned, if he were to join the two villages which lay below on either side of the Lot and fortify them he might create a place of safety, ease 'la *misère et la souffrance*' of his people and eventually fill his coffers.

The work was begun, but before they got round to the bridge itself Aquitaine had changed hands and it was Edward I of England who, in 1282, commanded that the bridge be started. It took seven years to build and was very beautiful, with five arches and three strong towers. It must have been well built as it lasted almost three hundred and fifty years until an enormous rising of the river carried it away. Today the bridge has only two arches of uneven width and the only sign of the towers is one huge base, which still remains.

There are two market days in Villeneuve. Every Tuesday and Saturday crowds pass through the medieval gateway to the colonnaded square in the centre. It is packed with stalls which, apart from the olive and nut and spice stall by the fountain, all sell fruits and vegetables, plants and flowers. There are large displays of every variety of salad, freshly cut batavia, curly endive, rocket, lambs lettuce, bunches of watercress a foot across. There are the long professional stalls aglow with perfect peppers, huge tomatoes, fat apricots, nectarines and early peaches from further south and the first scented melons. And there are the small stands, often just two wooden crates one on top of the other, where the local farmers' wives bring in their surplus produce. Here you can buy, if you are early enough, for they are the first to sell up and go home, their tiny beans, real fleshy tomatoes from the field, small courgettes, sprigs of thyme and basil, bunches of sweet onions and the occasional mixed spray of flowers from the garden. Their faces have become familiar and so it seems have ours.

'*Ah, madame, monsieur, vous êtes revenus au pays?*' – 'you've come back to the country?' – asks the little woman with the high sing-song voice who grows the best French beans. We admit it, admire her produce and stock up with as much as we can carry. As we leave the market we can't resist a voluptuous, pink, hanging begonia, for our porch. Almost a metre across, it gets heavier and heavier as we walk back to the car park. We stow our shopping in the car, carefully pulling the blind to shade the begonia, and return to sit and drink at the Café Tortoni and watch the world go by.

A canvas-covered jeep suddenly backs onto the pavement outside the estate agent next door to the café. A group of middle-aged men of various shapes and sizes in white shirts and dark trousers jump out and begin to unload music stands, instrument cases and, last of all, a tall cardboard box. The stands arranged, the instruments unpacked they amuse themselves by diving into the box like a lucky dip, and taking out a selection of straw hats and trying them on. A tiny sax player in shades, black hairline moustache and two-tone shoes, a French version of Sammy Davis Junior, disappears under a very large brim to much laughter.

Where to sit? Shade, under the estate agent's awning, is at a premium. The drummer, likely to be the most energetic, claims first choice and sets up his kit against the wall in the far corner. More musicians arrive. By 10.50 the two trumpets, one of whom appears to be the leader, are seated and blowing gently, finding their lip. Suddenly there are three trumpets, and two trombones. They are coming from all directions. Another sax player, as large as the other one is small, sits beside him and unpacks his instrument. What time are they due to begin? Eleven o'clock? They seem in no hurry. We order another drink.

As eleven sounds from the clock tower over the great *Porte de Paris,* a third trombone is greeted by the assembled players, all adjusting their chairs, and blowing little runs and trills. The shady spaces are almost gone and the sun growing stronger. Just as we think they must be complete, the euphonium player makes a spectacular late entrance befitting the size of his gleaming instrument. He is accompanied by his wife who, seeing him settled, takes the car keys and disappears only to return with a tambourine to sit next to the leader. After another exchange of hats and more ribaldry, Sammy Davis seeming a willing butt, the leader at last taps for attention and counts four.

They start with a *paso doble*. It is such a relief that they've actually begun that it takes a moment to realise that they are not very good. But they are loud. The crowds, pouring through the archway into the boulevard, are momentarily startled and slow down to listen. Some put down their shopping, and fold their arms, others walk on with heads turned to look back. There are a few collisions, for many carry great pots of flowers, canna lilies a metre high, morning glories trailed up a wicker pyramid, giant hibiscus in pink and white. They grin at the musicians who play determinedly on and on, hardly a pause between each number, the music unfamiliar but predictable.

The temperature rises, the players mop their brows, tilting back the straw boaters. The wife disappears again and returns with a large bottle of Evian. The euphonium drinks first. There is the briefest of pauses before they flip over their laminated dots clipped to the stands and, after a count of three, off they go again. This time it is a waltz and a pair of middle-aged women at the next table get up to dance. The crowd is beginning to enjoy it. As some drift reluctantly away, mindful of chores to be done, others take their place. The sun blazes down. The strip of shade is diminishing. The thought of our cool, blue pool urges us to return home and, as we leave, the proprietor of the Café Tortoni emerges, to a round of applause, with two extra umbrellas to give those on the outside edge a little extra shade. We go home to swim and eat cucumber salad and a large and succulent-looking quiche, which we've bought from the *charcuterie*.

CHAPTER FOUR

The last time we managed a spring visit was in 2001, when we tried a new route, flying very cheaply from Stansted to Bordeaux. The coach ride from Victoria to Stansted felt rather elderly and stately, but I actually enjoyed seeing London from such a high point of view. I also enjoyed the lack of responsibility for getting there on time. It is a long way and we were in the very competent hands of a fresh-faced, chatty, driver, wearing an earring. We Buzzed to Bordeaux; no-frills flying. In fact there was just as much space as on a flight to Antigua, to which we had treated ourselves a few months before, and considerably less junk; no pillows, socks, earphones, or blanket to juggle with, and no tightly wrapped condiments and cutlery to enrage one, only to be dropped, irretrievably, on the floor or down one's shirt. This time we simply chose from a tray of delicious sandwiches, which were so well filled that we found it enough to share one, deciding to keep the other to eat later. Alas, we had temporarily forgotten the foot and mouth epidemic. We were not allowed to take our sandwich off the plane. Firm but unexpectedly generous, the stewardess refunded the cost of the uneaten sandwich.

Our hire car was almost brand new and it was wonderful to be motoring once more along the uncluttered French roads. That April was unusually cold with bustling clouds in a bright blue sky. When we arrived at the house we were thankful that our friends Hugh and Sally had switched on our one, rarely used, electric fire and lent us another one to heat the bedroom. We laid a great wood fire for the morning and put hot water bottles in the bed before going down to the farm for our evening meal.

The first meal of the holiday in the warm kitchen where we have been so generously fed over the years is always special. We drink *pastis* or a home made *apéritif, vin de noix* or *vin de pêche* or, my favourite, *quinquina*

Here is the recipe, which was given to Claudette by a friend with family in Italy.

QUINQUINA

Ingredients: Four Seville oranges, one sweet orange and a lemon, a vanilla pod, and a kilogram of sugar.

Cut the fruit into quarters and macerate all for forty days in three litres of red wine and three quarters of a litre of *eau de vie*. Strain, bottle and leave for six months.

We, too, now make *quinquina* in London.

We began the meal with *le tourin*, the special soup of the region. The first time we tasted this garlicky broth topped with bread and melted cheese, we had been aroused in the middle of the night to taste it, with half the village, including the mayor, in our bedroom, but that's another story and one that I have already told. This time the soup was not, said Claudette, *fabrication maison*, but was apparently left over from *le repas des chasseurs*, the hunters' reunion of the previous evening. Raymond's eyes shone as he described the meal they had eaten, especially the *salade de gésiers*, bits of preserved duck gizzard, which followed the soup. He then extolled the next course, a *civet de chevreuil*, jugged venison, which was followed in turn by yet more venison, this time a roasted haunch, then came the *fromage*, and, to complete the feast, a tart; no doubt all washed down with excellent wine. Clearly there had been soup left over that evening, perhaps in anticipation of all that was to follow, and Claudette had simply brought it home. Nothing is ever wasted here. We, *chez* Claudette, followed the remains of the hunter's soup with a delicious salad; golden-yolked eggs, tomatoes, sweet onions, potatoes and a smidge of tuna, everything fresh and delicious. Our hostess then produced an *omelette aux asperges,* followed by roast guinea fowl and potatoes sautéed with garlic.

As we discussed current affairs on both sides of the channel, Raymond declared himself perplexed by the approach to the problem of the outbreak of foot and mouth, then at its height in England. He couldn't understand the wholesale slaughter.

'*La fièvre aphteuse,*' as it is called in France, '*c'était toujours là,*' he said. 'It's always been around. If an animal got sick we treated it. Sometimes we used *poudre de cuivre,* or something else...*c'était quoi,* Claudette?'

Claudette frowned. 'It's all so long ago. *Grezille* was it called?'

'*Oui. C'est ça,*' said Raymond. 'The same stuff they used to use when they shoed an oxen. And we used *chaux vive,* quick lime, to wash our boots. We did isolate the sick animal but it was very rare for any of the others to catch it. If it got better, which it usually did, *tant mieux,* so much the better. If it remained feeble...well, off to the abattoir, but...killing the whole herd,' he threw up his hands *'Jamais! C'est de la folie!* Mind you,' he added gloomily, 'until ten years ago we did vaccinate against it. Then – *les gens de Bruxelles,'* his face made it quite clear what he thought about them, 'they changed their minds. It was Britain and America who persuaded them. It's the large industrial farms that cause all the problems.'

'Comme toujours!' said Claudette, carrying in an enormous flan.

She then proceeded to tell us just what she, as a working farmer, thought about common market regulations. Each year she hand-rears one calf, which stays with the mother and is only given a supplement of cereal to augment the mother's milk. This calf provides the family with veal for the next year. Now, apparently, she had just been told that the latest regulations meant that after slaughter, the abattoir would return to her neither the brains, the intestines or the sweet breads; all the specially prized delicacies which she loves to cook and for which she has many special recipes.

'Même pas pour la consommation familiale!' she cried indignantly. There was a gleam in her eye, which suggested that she intended to find a way round this next year.

A few days later the carcasse of her special calf came back from the slaughterer and we went down to watch it expertly butchered by Robert, Grandma's cousin. In his long life he has been both a butcher and an *inséminateur,* and now, in his busy retirement, he is an enthusiastic beekeeper. He drives an old Post Office van, which has been repainted with VIVEZ MIEUX! MANGEZ DU MIEL! in large letters on the side. On market days he chauffeurs the little bus, which takes the old folk from his village to market. Today he was *le boucher.*

The operation was to take place in Grandma's kitchen where, so long ago, I sat to pluck my first and only duck. I can clearly remember the weight and the scent of its still-warm body on my lap, and the quiet amusement of Claudette and her mother at my squeamishness. Today, for the calf, the kitchen is all prepared. The long table is covered with scrubbed oil-cloth, another smaller wooden table placed at right angles. Already at the far end of the table lies the pallid head of the calf, the long-lashed eyes closed, the pale, thick, protruding tongue curved upward.

Robert greets us. Almost eighty now, his great jowls a little slacker, his sturdy frame just a little lighter, his eyes are still as bright as ever behind his small, round spectacles. He sharpens his knives with a flourish, his one-shouldered butcher's apron securely tied and reaching almost to his ankles. He places the knives precisely then goes outside to help Raymond. Together they stagger back in with the half-carcass. It seemed a small animal when alive; dead, even half of it seems enormous. And after all the bureaucratic fuss about brains and sweet breads and intestines I am astonished to see the gleaming spinal cord, considered in England a possible source of BSE, running the length of the body. Claudette dismissed my enquiry with a *'Pouff'* – there were more important things on hand.

As Robert deftly chopped and sliced, each cut of palest pink meat had to be carefully wrapped in tough yellow plastic bags for the *congélateur;* first *le filet,* then *les côtelettes,* followed by the tougher cuts for *pot au feu.*

'And don't forget to make me a little slit in each piece,' she insisted. 'To put in my *farce.'* She makes her stuffing with bread, egg and garlic. Robert's mobile eyebrows twitched but he obliged, using the tip of his knife with extreme delicacy. As each section of the calf was cut up the possible dishes were discussed that could be concocted from *'une bonne escalope, un jarret de veau, une demie épaule'.*

'Could you not roast a half-shoulder as you might with a lamb?' I enquired. They considered momentarily then shook their heads. *'C'est meilleur en casserole avec des petits légumes,'* they agreed.

Robert too, was bemused by the English reaction to *la fièvre aphteuse,* the foot and mouth.

'I remember '46 and '47,' he said. *'C'était l'épidemie mais,'* his eyebrows shot up. 'One or two might be infected. They might even lose a toenail – that was the worst – *mais...jamais le reste du cheptel l'attrapait. Jamais!* Never the rest of the herd.'

'Just what I told them,' agreed Raymond.

Robert tapped his nose. *'C'était un complot, un complot des marchands,'* – a plot by the wholesalers, he said, darkly. *'Il y a trop de viande dans les grands congélateurs* – there's a meat mountain. *Si vous tuez beaucoup de bêtes, vous pouvez vendre les autres* – if you dispose of all the live ones you can sell what you already have in the freezer.'

'And it's the small farmer who suffers every time,' said Raymond, *'comme toujours.'*

It did get warmer that spring but it also got wetter. We took Raymond and Claudette out to Sunday lunch to try a new restaurant, *Le Moulin de Labique.* In spite of the rain, which had just begun, the setting of the old mill was very picturesque. We were rather alarmed when we first entered to find that we were the only customers, but we had hardly sat down when a party of fourteen arrived and the room soon hummed with discussions of the menu. Once again, in this region of good food, we marvelled at the choice and the value for money. The days of five courses for 80 Francs had gone forever but, for 150 francs, at that time about £15, there was a choice of three starters, one of which was a salad with semi-cooked *foie gras.* The main dishes included a *roti d'agneau* with orange and ginger, *un civet de cannette* with *tagliatelle,* or *magret de canard* – duck breast – with a honey and shallot sauce. As usual we all had something different.

The lamb was especially good and the portions were generous. Claudette enjoyed herself, tasting everything. She loves to eat out and is much more adventurous than Raymond, who prefers to stick to what he knows. The desserts included *gratin de poire avec eau de vie de poire* and a homemade *mousse aux framboises,* so I was happy. And we drank a good bottle of Bordeaux for 10 francs.

The patron was in the process of restoring the rest of the building and took us on a tour to show us the beautiful tiled staircase leading up to the accommodation above. We wished him well. There are many such enterprising ventures, which begin hopefully, but the season here is short – mid-July to the end of August, as far as the French holiday-maker is concerned. Even *les étrangers* are heading homeward by the end of September. To make a good living all year round one must attract and keep local wedding parties and reunions, and the competition is fierce.

We ran to the car park, the rain even heavier now and clearly settled in for the afternoon. But Sunday is Raymond's day off. *'On va rendre visite a Ursula, peut-être?'* he asked eagerly. *'Je voudrais bien voir sa petite maison.'* Ursula had recently sold her very large farmhouse with extensive outbuildings and had moved to a smaller house. She always welcomed visitors, but I knew that she had broken her wrist during the winter and I wondered if we might find her a little frail. She was, after all, well over eighty. Braving the rain and up to her ankles in mud, she waved as we stopped the car. Her short, stylish hair with its blonde streaks was crammed under a sou-wester. She had just finished mucking out her two horses.

We crowded into her snug little house, hung with all the rosettes she has won for riding competitions. It is just across the courtyard from that of her daughter Susan, who came in briefly to greet us before dashing off again through the rain as she was preparing a meal for fourteen that evening. They are a formidable pair. Ursula showed us the photographs taken the previous summer when Susan had brought her mother back to England for a surprise party. Susan's brother had organised everything and the large and extended family had decorated a barn and crowned Ursula, 'Queen of the Summer'.

'And the wrist?' I enquired. 'Is it better?'

She flexed her arm. 'What a nuisance it was,' she said. 'But I've almost forgotten about it now.'

'Elle est indefatigable!' said Raymond as we left.

It rained the next day and the day after. A frog took shelter in the bathroom. There were lakes on either side of the house and, with the incessant rain, an inevitable drop in temperature. We kept the fire constantly burning. On a brief trip for supplies we were splashed by a council lorry, carrying large and ominous road signs. *ROUTE INONDÉE*. Getting the garden into shape, one of the main reasons for our visit, was out of the question and I consoled myself by listening to *France Musique,* the French equivalent of Radio Three, while polishing the furniture. It gave me pleasure to look at the newly plastered wall in the main living room, which our gentle giant M. Duparq had finished at the end of the previous summer. Only the bottom half had needed replastering and the new work was skilfully blended with the rough finish above it. While removing damaged plaster around the window he had unearthed some very attractive edging stones and had waited until we returned from shopping before covering them up again. When we decided to leave them exposed he was pleased and pointed them with great care.

We first became acquainted with M. Duparq when we needed someone to build a small, stone wall to edge the terrace by the newly dug swimming pool. Although he was highly recommended, we were unsure at first for he hardly spoke, apart from a sort of breathy *'Hmm,'* through his nose, as he gazed down from his great height at the job in hand. We soon learnt, however, what a skilled craftsman he was and, when we can afford it, have used him many times. He loves stones and is sensitive to old houses, and that has been essential when having any work done at Bel-Air. We have been determined, if possible, to *conserver le style* of this very old, simple house.

The most recent part of Bel-Air was built sometime just before 1889 when my predecessor Anaïs came here as a young bride. At that time, Justin's two brothers and her father-in-law were all living there. The new and highly necessary addition consists of two adjoining bedrooms and a continuation of the attic above just tacked onto the east side of the original house, which is much older. I suspect that this older part was once just one large, simple space with an attic above. In the centre of one wall is the chimney, two meters wide and resting on oak corbels. On the adjoining wall is set a sink, hand-cut from a single slab of granite, which drained water to the outside. On the opposite wall two window openings are cut, one above the other, a stone transom between them. They had no glass but each closed with its own oak shutter, much-mended and studded with great iron nails like the ancient door of the church. A small glazed window frame was added later in the bottom section but the top opening remains as it was.

The light from this window would have made it possible to climb the crude, uneven stairs to the attic. This is where the family must have slept, long before Justin, the eldest son, grew up and married Anaïs. I can imagine his father, Pierre Costes, a former weaver, now presumably working the land, chasing his three sons up to bed in the 1870s. Their mother died in childbirth when the youngest boy was only five years old. They also used the attic for storage, for we found piles of old corn-cobs, wine bottles, ancient wooden hay forks and crude teasing and carding tools. Downstairs, the opening on the west side of the building was originally large enough for a small cart to enter and the animals probably also came in when the weather was cold.

Of the actual date of the building there is no record, even in the Archives in Agen. So many documents were destroyed during the revolution. Some old deeds that have survived we found in the attic in a battered, cardboard hat-box. It was on the top shelf of an ancient sideboard pushed right to the back of the more recent addition. Mouse droppings and dead insects fell out as we gingerly unfolded the stiff packets of paper with their spidery writing. They do not tell us anything about our house, but those documents that didn't immediately fall to pieces and are just possible to decipher give intriguing glimpses of long ago life, not at Bel-Air itself, but not far away, in the same commune.

The earliest document is dated 1765 and records the troubles of one Sieur Antoine Larroque. He has fallen behind with the repayment of a loan of twenty-five *livres,* sixteen *sols,* to one Jean Domengie, who takes him before the tribunal in Monflanquin, the cost of going to the tribunal being thirty-six *sols. Livres,* and *sols,* are pre-Revolution coinage and date from Roman times. The smallest coin was a *denarius* and it is from these three coins that our own pre-decimal money, L,s,d, was named. When the Normans came to England they used their own coins, which were marked with a star. Norman French for star being *'esterlin,'* this was the origin of 'sterling'.

Antoine Larroque also had to pay interest on his debt, and his land and goods were to be mortgaged. He must have worked hard for the next document confirms that within three years he has paid it all off. His only liabilities now are taxes to be paid to King Louis XV and to the *Seigneur* of the local chateau. There is also mention of his owning some fallow land, which he gained from his wife's dowry. This land is further south and west in the department of *les Landes.*

A later but almost indecipherable document details the responsibilities of his son, who, post-Revolution, is now addressed as *Citoyen* Pierre Larroque. In a flourishing script it begins, *'Au nom de la République française, Salut, savoir faisons que...'*

Interestingly, this document is dated *Premier Ventôse* (very roughly the end of February) *Cinquième année de la République,* using the new Republican calendar, which was instituted in 1793. The Republican year began at the Autumn equinox on the 22nd September and was divided into twelve months of 30 days each. The problematic five or six days left over by this calculation were to be simply dealt with by being dedicated to Republican holidays. The names of the months are fascinating and often poetic.

Autumn is divided into *Vendémiaire, Brumaire, Frimaire.*

Winter becomes, *Nivose, Pluviose, Ventôse.*

Spring is *Germinal, Floréal, Prairial.*

Summer consists of *Messidor, Thermidor, Fructidor.*

So, according to this post-Revolution document, *Sieur* Antoine Larroque is now dead and his son, Citizen Pierre, is concerned with the enlargement of the room in which his father died. Also mentioned are his responsibilities to care not only for his mother but also his mother-in-law. There is also another document confirming that he has received fifty francs, the new money, in cash from his brother Jean, who will now take over the land inherited from their mother. Why these documents were brought to and kept at Bel-Air I shall probably never know. I imagine that the old sideboard, in which they had lain for so many years, was put up in the attic when the tall, heavy sideboard we use now, the new *buffet,* was bought. Perhaps the new sideboard was Anaïs's wedding present. Perhaps she brought it as her dowry. According to Sylvie's grandmother, Anaïs was very proud of her *buffet* and always kept it well polished. I give it an extra shine.

It did eventually stop raining during that spring holiday and work began again in the sodden garden. I planted up pots of morning glories and hoped that it would at least rain again before July to germinate them. We congratulated ourselves that even after thirty-six hours of a non-stop downpour, our house was as dry as a bone. That was until we went into the *chai,* our large outhouse. A *chai* faces north and fulfils the same purpose as a *cave,* or cellar, being a cool place to store wine. Our house is presumably built on rock, which would have precluded excavating. The *chai* is large, roughly fifty square metres, of which we have divided and converted half to use as a fourth bedroom. Not having any guests this holiday, we hadn't actually been in there. The shutters were still closed. The bed, covered with a plastic sheet, was fine but, as our eyes adjusted, we suddenly realised that all the rugs were moving, floating in three inches of water. Two dead mice swirled gently between them.

We grabbed every available mop and pushed the water and the corpses out. We had only just finished by the time Hugh arrived for supper. We cooked veal cutlets from the famous, family calf, on the griddle over the fire but, sadly, they were not very tasty.

The next day we looked for the leak in the *chai.* Where exactly had all this water come in? Dirty stains on one area of the wall gave us a rough clue. Mike, ever ingenious, drilled a hole through the pine panelling on the ceiling inside and by poking up a wire we gradually narrowed down the area outside on the long, sloping roof. We lifted and replaced the tiles carefully, one after the other. It took much patient investigation to eventually locate the cracked stop-tile. In the process of removing it, we found a chicken leg, picked clean, no doubt left by the *fouine,* when she was in residence. Whose chicken it had been would remain a mystery.

CHAPTER FIVE

On Sunday the weather was still very hot but the air was heavy, and by evening there was just a suggestion of something brewing on the other side of the horizon. We had spent a lazy day alone. We swam and lay in the shade, ignoring the piles of garden rubbish that would soon, if the strong young men appeared as they had promised, be cleared for us. Raymond and Claudette had taken a few days holiday in that period which they call here *'entre la paille et la prune,'* when the wheat is cut and the straw baled, but before the preparations must begin for the first plums to be harvested. They had gone to Cap d'Agde, where Véronique and Jean-Michel, their son-in-law, together with some of his five sisters, had bought a small apartment overlooking the harbour. We are thankful to escape from London to our rural idyll in Lot-et-Garonne; some of those who live and work in this wonderful space and quiet choose, for their diversion, a crowded, modern port.

While they are there Claudette will still do most of the cooking and Raymond will, as usual, get up very early, but only in order to explore all the surrounding area by bicycle. He has always loved to travel, taking advantage of the annual trips organised by the *Syndicat Agricole* to look at the differences in farms in various departments of France and abroad. This idea of taking a few days off from time to time by themselves, however, is new and is gradually establishing for them both a more agreeable kind of life. Raymond had long been worried about becoming too old to work the farm and the idea of future leisure seemed impossible. Now, Jean-Michel takes on increasing responsibilities and, although not from a farming background, proves himself more than capable, although their frequent disagreements about the right way to do things, *'les systèmes,'* can clearly be heard across the fields even over the roar of the tractor.

As Jean-Michel did ten years ago, Raymond married into the farm, but unlike Jean-Michel, Raymond's parents had always worked the land. In spite of this, he had to endure many a ticking off from Grandpa, Claudette's father. On becoming part of the household, Raymond, always polite, would sit at the table, continue eating and fume quietly while the old man roared his disapproval of the new and less than traditional way he had sprayed the plum trees or treated the vines. Claudette, tactfully, would not take sides. Jean-Michel is neither tactful nor deferential. He is confident, gives as good as he gets and confounds Raymond by, as well as having become a competent farmer, being also able to build and decorate, repair and weld machinery and still find time to play football. It just seems rather unfair that Raymond should have had to endure criticism from first the older and now the younger generation.

As we often do at the end of the day we walked slowly up through Raymond's newest vineyard toward the wood. When we first came, in those early days, going for walks to gaze at the view was a rare luxury, so much needed doing in the house. Now, after twenty-five years, there are changes even in the view. Then, the lower half of this long slope was still a meadow, bright with buttercups. A dozen of the large cream-coloured cows, *les Blondes d'Aquitaine,* would graze quietly here before trailing down at regular intervals to drink at the pond, and the wood itself extended further down towards Bel-Air. Over the years the lower half of the wood has been gradually cleared and the top section of the land ploughed, leaving a smaller but adequate pasture for the cows, who still come down to gaze at us solemnly when we first arrive. One glorious summer this top field was planted with sunflowers, and with *le grand champ,* as Raymond always calls it, on the other side of our house also a blaze of gold, we were, indeed, 'a house in the sunflowers'.

Plans for planting this new vineyard took a long time to come to fruition. The first we knew about Raymond's intentions was when, one spring, several years ago, he asked Mike to help him measure out the field for vines. Sunflowers seemed to be temporarily out of favour with Brussels and the thought of having a vineyard that we would be able to see from our front door was appealing. Back and forth the two of them trudged with canes three metres long. When they finally returned, exhausted, to sit and drink, Raymond appeared slightly alarmed to find that there was space for over 3,000 vines, which would also need the same number of stakes to support them.

Mike had sometimes been on stake-choosing expeditions with him in the past, and the cutting and trimming of the small acacias, the favoured tree, was quite arduous. They had never needed anything like 3,000!

There was also, it seemed, unlimited bureaucracy attached to the purchase of new vines. After permission actually to plant a new vineyard was finally obtained from *Le Bureau de Viticulture* in Bordeaux, Raymond learnt that no new licences to buy vines were being issued. All he had succeeded in obtaining was permission to buy up old licences. To plant even a single vine, never mind 3,000, he had to find growers who still had unused licences, usually because their vines had been uprooted and the land cleared. Raymond spent many months buying a few at a time, a licence for 50 vines here, another for 200 somewhere else. He would set off, confident of a bargain, having spoken to an elderly proprietor on the phone, only to find that by the time he got there the farmer had had second thoughts, or had discussed it with his sons, and the price had risen. The best deals were to be done when an old person had forgotten all about his licence, only valid for seven years, and had almost, but not quite, let it expire, which would have made it worthless. This lengthy process entailed many carefully planned visits around the region and Raymond enjoyed his quest.

When we returned that summer of '95 the sight of the great expanse of bare earth studded with strong, newly cut stakes was brutal. Each row of stakes was hammered through a wide strip of black plastic to prevent any weeds overwhelming the tender new vines, which could not be treated for the first three years. We had arrived just in time, for planting was to begin the following day. We were part of a willing but somewhat inexpert team on that sultry morning, as a co-opted pastry cook, a technical college lecturer, a Portugese welder, and Mike and I followed Raymond's instructions and carefully placed the small plants into the holes, turning the slender stems to curve towards the stake. As we worked, Jean-Michel roared up and down in the van, keeping us supplied with ever more plants.

Now those same vines are eight years old, strong and lush. We can see this year's grapes, still fairly small, already tightly packed on twisting stems. In the early morning light the long, neatly trimmed rows make dark tunnels. As the sun moves round, the shadows narrow and disappear, and by the evening, the tops of the rows are burnished. They are planted a metre apart to allow space for them to be harvested by machine. The few exceptions that we must still pick by hand are those vines nearest to the electricity pole, one of a line of poles, which march across the landscape, the cable providing perches for hunting kestrels and buzzards.

The first time the tall, unwieldy machine bumped up the track to harvest the new vines Raymond was very nervous. A large empty trailer stood ready for the grapes. Raymond and the driver of the machine, a small, disgruntled gnome of a man, eyed each other warily. No, he did not want anyone to help. He wasn't too happy to see me either, especially with a camera, and when he began to work we soon understood why. He was incredibly clumsy. At that time there were not many vines harvested by machine in this area. The driver was clearly inexperienced and consequently the last thing he needed was an audience. The mechanical battering and stripping of the grapes is a rough, cruel affair anyway; with this operator it was painful to watch.

At the end of each row he turned the machine so inexpertly he almost ripped the last vine from the ground. The whole noisy apparatus swayed and tottered astride each row and every time he unloaded into the trailer, grapes and leaves spilt all over the place. Raymond threw his arms into the air and cursed. Of course it was all very quick. The vineyard is so wide and the rows so long, a score of pickers would have taken several days to complete the harvest. But they wouldn't have made such a mess of it, or lost so many grapes. We were all relieved when the assault was finished. Thankfully we never saw this self-styled expert again and the following year the operator was much more sympathetic and skilful.

As we continue our walk we reach the edge of the wood and turn back to look at Bel-Air. It nestles into the landscape, the long slope of the roof just visible through the branches of the great ash tree in front. The Mediterranean cyprus on the other side of the house barely reached my chin when we planted it. Now, for the first time, I realise I can clearly see it from this side too, grown so tall that it appears like an exclamation mark above the roof. The little pine that Grandma dug up in the wood so long ago and carried down to plant for us is now a huge tree. She was always planting different things in our garden, sometimes in very inappropriate spots. Like many French gardeners she was a stickler for even spacing. Neat rows of zinnias or French marigolds would, with us away so much, soon be overwhelmed with weeds. Other offerings were inspired. I have two small rose bushes and the beautiful peony she planted for me in a perfect position, which seems to grow larger every year.

Grandma died in '97. Parkinson's disease, which she endured so bravely, finally reduced her to a shadow. Each October when we said goodbye we wondered whether the old people, both well over eighty, would still be there the following spring. At the end, Claudette nursed each of her parents with a tenderness she rarely displays. Raymond's feelings are immediate and uncomplicated, every emotion unashamedly expressed. Claudette is sharper, more protective of any inner vulnerability. She is like her father. Grandpa Jean would roar and rage, but he was the kindest, fairest man. He just didn't want anyone to know it. I miss them both.

So many times Grandma and I sat together, either up at Bel-Air or down on the farm, shelling white coco beans for bottling or cutting up greengages to make jam. Stick in hand, she would walk slowly up through the wood to Bel-Air in her flowered pinafore and wide straw hat. She would always carry a gift, a small bunch of parsley, a couple of sweet onions, or a bunch of sorrel to make soup. She was a very quiet person but sometimes she would talk about her childhood. Her parents died when she was small. She and her brother, who were very close in age, were brought up by a much older, married sister. The family owned and worked quite a large mill, but by the time Grandma and her brother had grown up, the sister's husband had squandered all the money. The mill and all the land had to be sold. Grandma's inheritance is now a flourishing, four-star campsite owned by a Dutch company. We used to make the occasional nostalgic trip on a Sunday after lunch, to see how it had been altered.

Sometimes Grandma would tell of her courtship, of how Grandpa would call to take her dancing on a Saturday evening. I imagine them setting off proudly in the Citroën, she, without a doubt, the envy of all the local girls. In the late twenties not many young men had a car. She was very pretty, with dark curly hair and very small hands and feet. Grandpa certainly didn't pick her as a sturdy wife for a farmer. He too was slightly built with a mop of fair hair. They were married in 1931 and she came to live at the farm. I don't think she got on too well with Grandpa's difficult and possessive sister, who lived in the next village. But with the war, all petty disputes were put aside as the whole community faced real hardship, especially when, with Claudette still very small, Grandpa, conscripted into the French army, was captured and spent five years as a prisoner of war in Germany.

'*Ah oui,*' she would sigh. '*C'était dur! Très dur!*' And that was all. Grandma always preferred to talk about happier times.

We were shocked when we arrived that last summer to see her so changed. She was in a wheelchair. A long silk scarf was tied round her waist to hold her safely in. She was confused and incredibly thin and frail, a sad reunion for us. Adam, my elder son, his wife, Caz, and my two grandchildren, had arrived by car on the first of August. Elliot, then two years old, was carried, still sleeping, straight to bed. Six-and-a-half-year-old Thomas demanded food and then raced all round the garden whooping with joy. We finally persuaded him into bed and had just sat down to a very late meal when Jean-Michel appeared. With tears in his eyes he told us that Grandma had died an hour ago.

Mike and I went down to comfort a sobbing Véronique. Grandpa sat, his head bowed, his sister by his side. Raymond's brother and his wife stood as if uncertain what they should do. Claudette, dry-eyed, just kept repeating bewilderedly, 'She was all right when I put her to bed. *Elle a même pris un peu de bouillon* – a little broth.'

She shook her head as though she still could

not believe it – as though she had not been able to acknowledge her mother's clearly impending death.

'When I put her to bed, *elle était comme toujours,*' she began again as she led us to the bedroom. Grandma, her jaw tied up with a crepe bandage, now lay there in her best dress, the one she had worn for her diamond wedding, six years before. She looked so small. A rosary had been wound around her bony, work-weary, little hands. Our great sadness was mitigated by relief that this gentle old lady no longer had to suffer the indignities of her illness.

The following evening we were invited down for special family prayers. There were other family members; Philippe and Corinne had come from Toulouse, cousins from La Capelle. In a large rough circle we sat outside in the open-ended hanger, waiting for the *Curé*. We waited and waited. No one seemed to know what to do. There was such a deep sense of shared loss and sadness. Mike suggested that we hold hands and he said a brief prayer. The family seemed grateful. Still we waited. The absent *Curé* was not, alas, the sweet old priest who had officiated at both Philippe's and Véronique's weddings. This priest was fairly new and not particularly popular. He did nothing to improve his reputation that evening with a grieving family. He did not come.

Eventually Philippe decided that we would have to say our farewells without him. We crowded solemnly back into the bedroom where Grandma lay. Philippe stood at the end of the bed. He said a few loving words and then a *Pater Noster* and an *Ave Maria*. Grandpa's sister, ever acerbic, declared that it was ten *Ave Marias* that must be said. Claudette began, the others joined in and all the endless and, to me, pointless repetition of the prayers of my Roman Catholic childhood came flooding back. The confessions, when I scratched around for a sin or two to tell the priest. My bewilderment as to why four Our Fathers and six Hail Marys would make it all better, and the difficulty of getting any of my questions answered. Then I felt ashamed of the rebellious anger that had momentarily welled up in me. Dealing with death needs every comforting ritual. 'Holy Mary, pray for us sinners, now, and in the hour of our death,' indeed. We all lined up to kiss her. Grandpa stood back until last, and in Occitan, the old language that they often spoke to one another, he shouted at her, in the way the very deaf do. Then he embraced her and howled *'Addio'* and then I did cry.

It was a scorching day for the funeral, which was held the next day at 5.30 in the village church. We went early to help prepare and found that Mme Barrou, who keeps the keys, had decorated everywhere with a variety of vases filled with delicate pink cosmos, no doubt from her own garden. Mlle Bruet, was also there, plugging in her portable organ. She looked alarmed when she saw me as we had met some years before at a rehearsal for Véronique's wedding when I had expected her to play my accompaniment for an *Ave Maria* I was to sing. It was then that I discovered that she could only read the melody line, which she played with one hand. Fortunately, at that time, my friend Christina, an expert accompanist and stalwart improviser on even the most dire instrument was staying with us for a few days, and she kindly managed to record my accompaniment onto tape before she went back to England.

Now Claudette had asked me if I would sing the same *Ave Maria* for the funeral, as Grandma had so enjoyed it. Grandma herself had a sweet voice and had taught me to sing *Le Temps des Cerises*, Cherry Time, a great favourite with the older generation. I quickly reassured Mlle Bruet that I was happy to sing unaccompanied and left her to rehearse the small choir of elderly ladies in hymns all set, alas, as always, too high for them. The choir were very undecided about my solo. They shook their heads and fretted that perhaps it would be necessary to ask the *Curé*. It was quite likely that an *Ave Maria* would not be considered at all suitable for a funeral. I was determined to sing it anyway but when the *Curé* eventually arrived he shrugged and said loftily, '*Je ne vois aucun empêchement*, I see no obstacle.' I forbore to point out that I was singing it not for him but for Grandma. Sung in a lower key and much slower than for the wedding, the *Ave Maria* ended the simple service and felt right.

I was proud of Philippe who spoke movingly about his grandmother. He looked so tall and handsome and I remembered the slim, brown-legged boy who had come out, eager to greet us the very first time we had driven up to the farm. When the service was over we all wound our way through the village and up to the small cemetery where, after a long and hard life, this loving and much loved grandmother was laid to rest.

We walked slowly back home from the vineyard, the dying sun slanting through the poplar trees at the edge of the track before it disappeared, and we drank a toast to the two old people who had, over so many years, shown us such kindness.

CHAPTER SIX

Guy and his friend from university turned up as they had promised and dealt with our piles of garden rubbish, the speed and ease with which they worked making us feel very old. I had known Guy since he was a baby. In the following summers we had all been enchanted by this blonde toddler who loved to ride on Raymond's tractor and was fearless in our neighbour's pool. When he was about five years old I had watched his face change from excited apprehension to delight as he swallowed his first oyster. I did not imagine then that one day he would be over six feet tall and would take on those tasks which we could no longer manage.

They made short work of trimming our straggling hedge, restoring our view up to the vineyard and, as they pulled up the splendid growth of weeds behind the hedge, we discovered something else that we had forgotten; a neat stack of about two hundred, very old Roman roof tiles. That reminded us that we had still not found a solution to the roofing over the small terrace outside our fourth bedroom, which we had made in the *chai*. As long as the weather was fine, guests who stayed in that room were happy to walk outside to the shower. When it rained hard, however, they got a shower of a different kind and too often had also to negotiate a small lake. We left an umbrella just inside the bedroom door but year after year we puzzled about what to do.

The difficulty lay in the joining together of two roof edges, which sloped in different directions. 'There must be a solution,' said Mike after a particularly spectacular downfall, which threatened to reach the step of the *chai* and flood the room. He made a paper model, we began to see a possibility and felt at least one step nearer to getting the problem solved. Who would actually do the job was yet another problem. Then the previous summer we had had the chance to acquire some really old tiles. They had come from reroofed outbuildings at the local chateau, which we learnt had just been sold, and restoration work had begun.

From the first year that we bought Bel-Air we have known about the local chateau. On brief moments of respite in those early days, as we sat outside in the sunshine, with a hastily concocted sandwich and a glass of wine, the distant cry of peacocks would often drift up across the fields when the wind was from the south. Later, when we had more time and began to explore our region, on our way to our nearest town of Monflanquin, we would catch a glimpse through the trees of a large shuttered house with an elegant but crumbling loggia on one side and a high-turreted belfry. Although we could not see it, we knew that there was also a lake, because Grandpa, as the local *gardien de chasse,* had permission to fish it for trout and crayfish.

From various people we heard the sad story of Monsieur, the late owner of the chateau and the last in the line of the once proud family De Becay, who in happier times had been close to the Royal Court. The locals seem to have been fond of the old man, the sole survivor. They understood and respected his decision to remain unmarried and not to have children, fearing that any offspring might inherit the madness of his older brother. However, we learnt that, later in life, Monsieur did eventually marry a middle-aged widow with children of her own. One of the sons, the story said, became involved in Paris in a court case involving fraud, causing his stepfather a great deal of unhappiness. The years passed, Madame died, and Monsieur, now old, alone and frail, and presumably in financial difficulties, made, with the man who normally sold his sheep for him, a perfectly legal arrangement that is quite common here. It would, he hoped, assure him of an income for the remainder of his life, but as it turned out, it also provided a source of local gossip for years to come.

Raymond had, in fact, acquired Bel-Air in 1961 by a similar arrangement. *Rente viagère,* as it is called, is a life annuity agreement between an elderly person and a relative, or a trusted friend or neighbour. Simple and very practical, it is designed for people who reach a stage in their lives when they need support but do not wish to leave their home. Each agreement is an act, carefully drawn up by the *notaire* to suit each particular situation. In the case of our property, Raymond agreed that, after paying the sum of roughly one-and-a-half thousand pounds to Anaïs and her handicapped son at Bel-Air, he would provide them annually with a specified quantity of wheat, wine, potatoes, firewood and feed for the chicken. On the first death, all these amounts were to be halved, except the firewood. On the second death, Bel-Air, and more importantly to him the land, would be his.

After signing the agreement, Anaïs lived for another two years, and her son, Alois, lived on until 1968. For the last two years of his life he was too ill to live alone and moved to be cared for into the *maison de retraite,* but Raymond continued to support him in the nursing home and to take him his wine and tobacco. On Sundays he would bring him up to a now unoccupied Bel-Air to sit quietly and look at the view. Of course there are risks in such annuity agreements; the longer the seller lives, the worse the bargain. It is not completely unknown for some old people to actually outlive the potential benefactor.

Raymond's small gain, after seven years, of our modest house and a couple of fields was as nothing compared with the legacy of the chateau, which also included in the agreement another large house, the grandest in the village; as well as two more substantial stone-built farmhouses and a great deal of land. What our village has never got over is the fact that after entering into a life annuity agreement with his *marchand de moutons,* poor old Monsieur at the chateau was dead within a month! There is no serious suggestion of a crime having been committed, although there are shrugs and frowns and taps on the side of the nose, as the story is told and re-told. It is the incredible unfairness of it all that people bemoan and the fact that the now extremely wealthy sheep merchant, whom one might have expected to be the soul of contentment, is, apparently, an extremely difficult man. Monsieur T. had posted 'Keep Out' notices all round the chateau, it was said, although he himself had no intention of living there, having a large modern house elsewhere. It was also rumoured that he had installed explosive devices along the tree-lined drive, the entrance to which he had now blocked with a great fallen tree.

We first met this notorious *'marchand de moutons'* at the village fête. It was actually an alternative to the normal village fête. For several years the village had been split into two factions. One supported the mayor, who was interested in speaking Occitan and playing the fiddle; the other considered him to be both too radical and too exotic. The opposition included most of the local farmers, Raymond being prominent among them. Not wishing to take sides, for several years we ended up going to both fêtes. It was quite an exhausting business since they tended to be held on consecutive days, and entailed a great deal of eating and drinking. One year, however, they were held on the same day and we had to choose.

It was at this large gathering of recalcitrant farmers that we first met Monsieur T. He was a tall, confident man with a handsome, florid face. There was a great deal of local wine consumed and he was in an unusually mellow mood. The question of the future of the chateau was raised and the new owner told us that he was still looking for a buyer. Perhaps we would know someone in England who might like to buy it? Would we like to visit the chateau? Omitting to tell him that there were very few millionaires among our acquaintances, we naturally said yes. A small party, including Raymond and Claudette, left the fête and were taken on a tour. We parked on the opposite side of the road to the chateau, skirted the obstacle of the fallen tree and walked up the long, overgrown drive.

The great house was a sad and sombre place. The kitchen was still almost medieval, with massive oak cupboards stretching from the floor up to the smoke-blackened ceiling. In the vast, sooty fireplace remained the spit with the winding gear to turn the roast. A more recent addition was a row of bells to summon the servants, marked *Monsieur, Madame, Chambre Rouge, Chambre Verte, Lingerie.* The once elegant, marble-floored entrance hall was bare and dingy, and all the way up the wall of the wide staircase, pale silhouettes in the darkened plaster showed where ancient arms and armour had once been displayed. The faded wallpaper in the bedrooms was patterned with intricate oriental designs and each bedroom led into the one next door. The hand basins in the more important bedrooms were large and very much of their period, the bath was in one of the bedrooms, concealed behind tall wooden panelling which was painted a faded blue. In all this great house there seemed to be only one lavatory, tucked away on a small landing. I wandered outside and into the once elegant loggia, with its wooden balustrade, which overlooked the lake, now green and blocked with fallen trees. There were dusty punts drawn up, poles slotted into the roof, and I imagined lazy summer days of long ago, with laughter and young people in elegant clothes, fingers drifting in the water.

Over the years, as he sold some of the other properties, Monsieur T. began to spend money on the chateau. From a distance we noted that the loggia was being refurbished. New stonework was evident. The next year as we drove by we saw that the roof had been repaired. There was much discussion about the suitability of red tiles having replaced the original slate, and of the million pounds that Monsieur T. was rumoured to be asking for a sale. Each year speculation grew.

We had hardly arrived last summer when Véronique, Raymond's daughter, in her new capacity as deputy mayor, had called to ask if Mike and I would mind acting as interpreters. 'C'est vendu, le château! The chateau has been bought, by an Englishman,' she told us excitedly. He had apparently installed two English workmen on site who wished to register for a *permis de résidence,* and, not surprisingly, neither she nor the mayor could make them understand all the necessary formalities. Apart from being curious, we were happy to help our popular new mayor. Patrick Jayant is a young man with a wide, smiling face, whom I remember as a teenager always ready to lend a hand at the village celebrations, staggering around with great crates of food or drink. The best thing about him as far as the now united village is concerned is that he is a farmer. He understands.

We drove with Véronique to meet the mayor at the chateau and as we turned off the road saw that the once overgrown and sombre driveway was now trimmed and rutted by traffic. At the top of the drive two large mobile homes were drawn up between the house and the garden, connecting cables for power and water snaking through the grass and across the drive into the house. A pair of sturdy young men, Kevin and Pat, with their wives and children, came out to meet us. Kevin, who was in charge of the whole project, had worked in England for the new owner, a Mr Ensor, who had installed them there for as long as it would take to get the chateau back into shape. They seemed pleased at the challenging prospect, which they reckoned would take at least eighteen months, and now wanted to formally register as resident in France in order to send their children to school in September. Kieran and Kitty, Pat's children, who were about nine and seven, were clearly enjoying the whole adventure. Kevin's two little girls, who were much younger, seemed unsure. We translated for the Mayor and his very pretty deputy, as best we could. It seemed that a great many forms would have to be completed and we arranged to go with Kevin and Pat on the following Tuesday afternoon to the *Mairie,* that being the only time in the week that Odile the secretary is there.

We had expected some bureaucracy but as the two young men strove that afternoon to remember their wives' and even their mothers' maiden names it was clear that we were in for a long session. Birth and marriage certificates were needed and would have to be sent from England it now appeared.

Odile sighed. *'Oui, c'est tellement compliqué,'* she said, spectacles on the end of her neat little nose as she scribbled away in a large, official dossier. 'And all this material will have to go to the *Préfecture* at Agen. Your certificates in English have to be translated by a licensed translator and then, at the *Préfecture*, everything will be filed, I suppose,' she laughed. *'C'est tou jours comme ça.'*

'D'you think it'll be done by September, in time for the children to go to school?' asked Kevin. She nodded. *'Oh, Oui.* We can do with a few more children in the school.'

That evening we went into Monflanquin to listen to a concert in the square. We had already listened to a feast of music that summer. Sadly it was to prove the last time that *Musique en Guyenne* would enliven the last two weeks of July, but we were not to know that at the time. Every summer for the past seventeen years this wonderful festival of music-making to the highest standard had delighted large crowds of both local people and holiday-makers, many of whom deliberately chose those two weeks to come to Monflanquin.

There were master-classes in violin, guitar, brass and piano, with students coming from all over the world. At all hours of the day, music floated from the doors and windows of every available studio space. Lone instrumentalists sat quietly practising, high up on the ramparts overlooking the rolling countryside below. Over a hundred choristers who, for the past months, had been learning the score for that year's performance in their own small choirs all over France, were reunited and began rehearsals. Handel's *Messiah*, Faure's *Requiem*, a *Stabat Mater* by Dvorák, Haydn's *Creation*; each year the choir tackled something new and for the final rehearsal in the church the, always excellent, professional soloists arrived.

Each year the festival ranged ever wider for venues. Local chateaux welcomed us into their elegant courtyards for piano recitals, rarely used small churches were opened, spring-cleaned and filled with as many chairs as could be packed inside. There we might listen, at excitingly close quarters, to a string quartet, a guitar recital, or a small visiting choir from Romania. The acoustics were often amazing and the programmes imaginative. A few days earlier our local church had been favoured and the discomfort of our collection of hard and rickety chairs was forgotten, as we were treated to a series of Mozart sonatas for violin and piano. The violinist, from Vietnam, serene and sweet, with a ponytail, was also giving the master-classes; the

American pianist was flamboyant and dazzling.

At a cello recital in the tiny church of Lugagnac we had met Ursula. Her house is just nearby. We were glad to see her for we had heard that she was ill. She soon corrected us.

'I *was* ill,' she admitted. 'Pneumonia. Couldn't breathe – and now,' she sighed. 'They've discovered my blood pressure is too high. So I'm on medication to thin my blood. I mustn't cut myself. I said to my doctor, 'Well, can I ride?' He said, in his wonderful English – she imitated wickedly – 'You may ride, Madame, you may not fall off!'

She told us about her new puppy, which she clearly adores, and about her new mayor, whom she equally clearly does not. She had to see him because the dog had eaten some documents. *'Monsieur le Maire, je suis désolée mais mon chien a mangé ma carte de séjour,'* she had begun and then giggled. *'Madame, c'est très sérieux,'* he had thundered without a smile which, of course, she said, had made her laugh even more. I can't imagine Ursula ever having been pompous; now, well over eighty, she can be as frivolous as she likes.

Each year at the end of the first week of the music festival the students would give a free concert in the square. It was both a thank you to the little town for so warmly accommodating the annual musical invasion and a gentle encouragement to everyone to buy tickets for the rest of the concerts. For this concert we ate

supper early and drove into Monflanquin to be sure
of a seat close to the front. The young orchestra from
Westphalia, after what seemed an age of tuning up –
although nothing is ever done in a hurry here – started
off the evening with the Overture from *Oberon*. The
orchestra then took a short break while the concert
continued with a young Russian who bowed with
immense dignity before seating himself at the piano
and dashing off an impressively difficult piano solo
by Liszt. As the audience applauded and cheered his
performance, more and more people arrived, slipping
quietly into their seats. The light began to fade and arc
lamps were switched on. A chair was set in the middle
of the stage and a small Japanese girl carried in her
cello and sat very still for a moment before she began
to play Bach, her long thick hair swinging gently as
she tilted her head. There was a pause as the orchestra
returned and retuned. People changed seats for a
better view or to sit nearer friends. We then enjoyed
two young violinists who shared the Beethoven violin
concerto. The first player was French and she tackled
the very difficult first movement; the second and the
third movements, which run together, were played by
another Japanese student. It was fascinating to compare
their different strengths and weaknesses. The audience,
now grown so large that it was necessary for some to
find seats on the walls around the square, responded
with enthusiasm.

As the evening continued and stars began to appear, children gradually fell asleep and were carted home; their places taken by diners at nearby restaurants who, having finished their meals, came closer to listen. The small tree-lined square has a wonderful atmosphere, perhaps because for almost seven hundred and fifty years it has been a place for meeting and celebration. Just after midnight the orchestra, after many an encore, persuaded us to go home with the sound of their final spirited performance of Brahms' *Hungarian Dances* still ringing in our ears as we all drove away down the dark and winding roads.

A few days later we had to go to Bordeaux to meet Thomas. Our ten-year-old grandson was flying out to have a week with us on his own before the rest of the family arrived. Neurotic grandparents, we left at 8.30 a.m. to get to Bordeaux to meet the plane at 11.32. Bordeaux is only a hundred miles from us and as we sped along we discussed ways of passing the time after our inevitably very early arrival at the airport. All these ideas were forgotten as on the ring road into Bordeaux we encountered a five-kilometre tailback. We crawled past the road works, and frequent deviations, becoming increasingly worried. When we finally arrived at 11.30 we parked the car and raced into the reception hall to find a slightly tense Thomas, fortunately looked after by a friendly and conscientious air-hostess. Thomas was on his best behaviour. No doubt he had been primed by his parents and, without his brother, whom he really adores but...he was an easy and surprisingly grown-up and delightful young guest.

He had arrived in time to watch one of our trees being cut down. When we first bought Bel-Air there was one great ash tree, which gave us shade on the north side of the house. Nearer to the house, almost touching the wall of the *chai* was another ash, originally a seedling I suspect, of the older tree. It was small and graceful then and we didn't listen when Raymond tut-tutted and told us that it was too close to the house.

'*Il faut le couper, maintenant,*' he had said '*Autrement*...you're going to have problems one of these days.'

He was right, of course, he always is where growing things are concerned, and now the day of reckoning had finally arrived. The once small, graceful tree had become a towering hazard, its branches over-hanging our long sloping roof. Apart from any damage it would do if it ever fell, the constant cleaning out of twigs and fallen leaves from the channels between the tiles was an essential but irksome task. Mike had constructed a long pole with a hook at one end to tackle this, but in fact, he often had to also climb up on the roof to dislodge a particularly stubborn clump of moss, growing on its own perfect little compost heap of leaves. If these were left they would act as a dam and the rain would back up and eventually find a way through the tiles. One year we even had to uproot a couple of self-sown teazles actually flourishing on the roof.

We spoke to our friend Simone, who has a large garden with many trees, and she recommended the services of a Monsieur Bentoglio. We were sad to contemplate the felling of the tree but knew that it was essential. M. Bentoglio whistled when he first saw the height of it and the position but reassured us that it would present no problem, apart from costing us £320. Now, on the day of the felling, a team of four had arrived; Monsieur and Madame Bentoglio, their son and the man who seemed to be in charge of the lorry. He, it seemed, would do most of the cutting and work from the cabin at the top of the elevator arm. The main difficulty, apart from not letting heavy branches drop onto the roof, was the small space between the two trees in which to manoeuvre the elevator lorry. We did not want to damage our other tree.

It was fascinating to watch them work as a team. The lorry was constantly moved and jacked into different positions. The cutter dealt with the higher, smaller branches first, lopping and stacking them beside him in the elevator platform. When there was no more room on the platform he would lower himself, to where he could safely throw the branches down. He never threw anything without looking first and the others never moved without checking. M. Bentoglio picked the branches up. The son quickly chain-sawed them into manageable lengths, constructing a neat log pile as he did so, and Madame, in her neat spotted pinafore, raked and cleared the bits.

Minute by minute the shape of our very high tree changed as the top branches disappeared. As well as a power saw, the cutter also used a long, sharp lance for smaller branches and with this he would loop and tie a rope to secure and control heavier branches. At last there remained only the largest, most dangerous overhanging branch to remove. While M. Bentoglio hung onto the rope, his face red with the effort, the last great limb was severed and turned safely away from the roof, and finally M. Bentoglio himself ceremonially sawed through the trunk. Our tree was no more. Instead we had a neatly stacked pile of logs, the cut ends making a very pleasing design of varying circles. An equally tidy pile of small branches was left to dry alongside the barn. The ivy-covered trunk waited to be taken one day to the sawmill, and all that remained to remind us of the operation was a bright, sweet-scented ring of new sawdust. It took this organised and very professional team almost three hours and we reckoned they had earned their money.

While Kevin and Pat were hard at work transforming the chateau, their wives, Claudia and Diane, brought the children up to Bel-Air to swim. Thomas and Kieran immediately made friends and Thomas would return with him to go exploring the chateau and the grounds. One evening when I went to collect him, Kitty, Kieran's young sister, offered, with a delightfully proprietorial air, to take me on a tour. Although living very comfortably in their large mobile-homes, the children had made a playroom in the chateau. In the large reception room next to the kitchen, modern plastic toys and children's tricycles stood incongruously on the elegantly tiled but dusty floor. Dolls sprawled in a heap on a coloured blanket.

'Would you like to start at the top?' Kitty enquired. She led me not to the grand staircase, but up the winding back stairs. Up and up we went where I discovered eight more bedrooms on the top floor, which I had never seen. We peered out of the high windows, one giving a view down onto the lake, another onto the top branches of the great dark cedar trees below. In another of the rooms was a light well, like a small counter built over a glass panel in the floor through which one could see into the room beneath. I wondered why it was there, how many people had looked down through it over the years and what they had seen. On we went, up another small wooden staircase into the great wooden belfry.

'We'd better not ring the bell,' she giggled. 'The boys kept on doing it yesterday.'

We had heard nothing up at Bel-Air. Clearly the call of the peacocks, now long disappeared, had carried further than the sound of the bell.

'And now,' she said dramatically, ' I'll take you to see the bats.'

Back we went down the dark narrow staircase, ducked under a low doorway into the sculleries at the back of the kitchen, and she carefully pushed open a small metal door. 'You can just look,' she whispered, very seriously.

The bats, like a row of upside down very dirty, grey handkerchiefs, hung from the low ceiling.

Kitty put her finger to her lips. 'We mustn't disturb them,' she said closing the door again.

I wondered how much of all this Kitty would remember when she grew up, but before the summer was out her father had decided that he wasn't cut out to spend months, if not a couple of years, in rural France and she and her family left for home.

Preparations were in hand for the village fête to be held that Saturday. The new committee, which included Véronique, was still finding its feet. After the joining of the two opposing factions in the commune under the new mayor, it would take a few years it seemed, for the summer fête to regain its former glory. It was to be a smaller affair, held in the playground of the school, but Raymond made a special journey to the chateau to make sure that *'les Anglais'* were invited to book their places. And reminded that they must bring their own plates, glasses and cutlery. The day before the fête, I was surprised when Thomas offered to come shopping, until I saw him solemnly deciding in the supermarket which gel he should buy to make the front of his hair stand up. The next evening, although the sun had almost gone down before we left for the village, he put on his sunglasses and tried hard to look cool in his brand-new shirt. He and Kieran eyed the local girls but were soon racing around with the boys in the field behind the school. Tables were arranged in the playground, which is not particularly large as there are usually only about a dozen pupils in the school.

The evening began as always with unlimited aperitif, a very potent Sangria. Mme Renée, and Mme Barrou, who, for as long as I can remember, have been stalwarts of all preparations for village affairs, from fêtes to weddings and funerals, had at last taken honourable retirement. They sat at their ease with their husbands, while the younger generation served the first course which was, inevitably, generous portions of rice salad with tuna, hardboiled egg and sweetcorn. Raymond always leaves the sweetcorn. *'C'est pour les bêtes!'* he declares.

He knows perfectly well that maize grown for human consumption is a different variety but still refuses to try it. Many local farmers grow edible maize. The flowering plumes are more silvery and the foliage more delicate, but Raymond still cannot bring himself to eat it. He also won't eat broad beans, yet he adores '*soupe de fèves*'. Broad beans are for making soup and that is that. Mike adores broad beans and tells him how delicious they are eaten fresh. Raymond shrugs; '*Oui, c'est possible,*' he says with a shrug, '*mais une bonne soupe de fèves, comme celle de Claudette, ah!*' he kisses his fingers

Music for the disco started after the first course and people got up to dance. The smell of meat cooking was tantalising but it was ten o'clock before the trays and trays of barbecued lamb chops were passed, and repassed, interspersed with plates of sausages. There was no limit. The young men seemed to be vying to see who could consume the most of everything. After the meat, eaten with chunks of good bread, a green salad appeared and everyone took the obligatory leaf, except Claudia, Kevin's wife who, being a vegetarian, made the most of the salad, before a generous portion of cheese was served. As soon as one of the many bottles of red wine, from the local *Cave des Sept Monts* at Monflanquin, was finished another took its place. There were, by now, many flushed faces, but it could have been the dancing, of course. There was delicious apple tart specially made for the fête by the *boulanger* at the mill, and ice cream for the children, none of whom seemed the least bit tired.

In the course of the evening we caught up with local

gossip. Mme Vidal was going to retire, who would take over the village shop was as yet unclear. M. René, our now retired builder who had helped us so much in the early days had had a back operation but it had not been an unqualified success. He still had pain. Poor René. I remember years ago when he would whizz me round the dance floor at some fête or other. We chatted about the old days. *'Les beaux jours d'autrefois',* the nostalgic phrase that used to amuse us when we first came but which begins to have a meaning for us, too, now. Spurring each other on, the old folk shouted for me to sing *Le Temps des Cerises,* the song about cherries that grandma taught me. Unable to refuse, I sang and, responding to shouts, I also included something a bit more up-to-date for the young ones. I realised as I performed that Thomas had actually never seen his grandma on the end of a microphone before, with an audience. He gazed at me with a wonderful mixture of pride and embarrassment.

The English party from the chateau loved the fête, the food, the wine, the dancing and the relaxed and friendly atmosphere. Kevin talked about the work at the chateau, which was going well. That was when he told us about a quantity of old tiles he had replaced and for which there didn't seem to be a market. They were the handmade Roman tiles, larger at one end than the other. This is of course so that they can overlap, but these were so old that he had been told that they were probably made in the original way; the slabs of soft clay moulded over women's thighs. Perhaps this accounts for the slight variations. After I'd finished pondering on whether moulding soft clay over one's thighs would be a pleasant experience or not – I suppose like everything else it would depend on the weather – I remembered our perennial problem with the west corner of our house and our various schemes to roof it over. At least a stock of old tiles, which would blend in with our long sloping roof, would be one step nearer to a solution. When we all staggered home about midnight, we arranged to come and look at them.

A few days later we borrowed Raymond's *fourgonette* and made several trips to the chateau. I'd forgotten just how heavy Roman tiles are. It was many years since I'd helped with the reroofing of the west terrace. Then, once back at Bel-Air, we had to unload them. And there they still were under the weeds, in the neat stack that Guy and his friend had just uncovered. We resolved to put them to use before this summer was over.

CHAPTER SEVEN

One of our first ever visitors to Bel-Air was Guy's father, Hugh Fowles, a colleague of Mike's at Goldsmiths' College. Hugh and his partner Sally, en route to a tennis tournament at Bordeaux one summer, were curious to see exactly what kind of a place we had bought. In the 1970s, restoring an old property in rural France was not as popular a venture as it would later become, and many of our friends thought us quite mad to take on a house so derelict and entailing such a long journey south. When they actually saw Bel-Air, Hugh and Sally were much more sympathetic and on their return from the tennis at the end of that August, they called in again. We were already packing up to go home as our younger son, Matthew, had to return to school, but the weather was so glorious that they asked if they might stay on in our house. With anyone else I might have hesitated.

Closing up for the winter is quite a procedure. Water and electricity must be turned off, the heater tank drained, plastic covers put over the beds and sofas, just in case of a leaking roof after winter storms Garden furniture must be stored, mouse poison laid in all the rooms, the washing machine emptied, every shutter secured; the list goes on and on. But Hugh was so practical and when, after supper that evening, he had cleared the table and almost finished the washing up before I had drained my coffee cup, I had no doubts.

Hugh and Sally returned the following summer with seven-year-old Kym, Sally's daughter. A bright pixie of a child, she clearly enjoyed playing 'house' at Bel-Air. Hugh, the most competent and speedy craftsman I know, helped us solve the problem of our dark and draughty earth-floored corridor which led out onto the west side of the house. The opening had once been large enough to admit a farm cart, the arching wooden lintel still visible in the stones. The doorway had since been lowered but, with the heavy doors open, a prevailing wind would still almost blow one away. With the doors shut, however, the corridor was impossibly dark. Inner glass doors were clearly the answer but the only doors in Bricomarche, the local DIY shop, were out of the question. Eventually Hugh and Mike found a pair, which were just the right size and style, leaning amongst all the old materials in M. René, the builder's, yard. With Hugh's help and the necessary timber they were fitted in record time.

Hugh and Sally were delighted with our unspoilt region and began to consider the possibility of finding a ruin of their own to restore. Before they left that autumn, Raymond, who had already taken to them both, agreed to keep an eye out during the winter for anything suitable. When Mike and I arrived the following spring, Raymond, clearly pleased with himself, announced that he thought he just might have found something.

'*Ça n'a pas était facile,*' he declared solemnly 'You must realise there are not many *vieilles maisons en pierre,* old stone houses, left in the region.' Then he brightened. '*Mais, venez voir!*'

He took us to see quite a large house about three kilometres away, which had been part of a nearby farm. *Le patron,* whom Raymond knew, had on the death of his parents originally sold the house to an English couple. The husband and wife had then, apparently, fallen out, though whether over their French project was not clear. Nothing had been done to the house since the sale several years previously, and though not a complete ruin it was by now very neglected. The farmer had meanwhile used the main room for storage and for drying tobacco. Dusty strings hung disconsolately from the ceiling. The ex-wife of the vanished owner

– they were now divorced – was apparently living in Bangkok, which would make negotiations more difficult, and the whole place was smothered in ivy. Mike was apprehensive that the thickness of the ivy might well be the sole reason that the house was still standing but, as we had promised, we took pictures to show Hugh and Sally. Mike was at great pains to absolve himself of any responsibility should the whole enterprise prove a disaster.

As one end wall of the house collapsed before the protracted negotiations between London and Bangkok were completed, it very nearly was, but we should have had more faith in Hugh and Sally's ability and enterprise. Within a few years the ivy-covered ruin was transformed into a stylish and elegant house with a swimming pool. Hugh and Sally and their two children (Guy was born in '82) became regular visitors and unfailingly helpful both to us and to Raymond. Hugh moved from Goldsmiths' to York University and, as he and Sally began to find their hectic teaching schedules increasingly onerous, at the end of each summer holiday the idea of a complete change of career enabling them to live permanently in France, started to appeal.

Fifteen years previously, a M. Bernard Francoulon had just begun to fulfil his long-held ambition. As he had gazed around the farm, which he had inherited from his parents, his vision for the future was not of bumper harvests of maize or sunflowers, herds of strong, creamy cows, of planting strong new vineyards, or even of creating smart *gîtes* for holiday-makers. He had just one dream for his farm on the edge of the small town of Tombeboeuf, about half an hour's drive from us. To the utter astonishment of the whole neighbourhood he began the slow transformation of his parents' land into a golf course. The original farmhouse became the clubhouse, he kept the barns to store his machinery and, against all expectations, he succeeded in turning the whole property into a very attractive nine-hole course, with lakes and woodland, and also, in a region where golf was not then popular, he began to acquire a keen membership.

During the holidays Hugh and Sally and friends went occasionally to Tombeboeuf, to play at *le Golf de Barthe*. M. Bernard liked Hugh. He found him sympathetic. He was thinking of retiring, he said, as they played the course together. Not yet, of course, but, he shrugged, sometime in the future. As he grew older the running of the whole affair was becoming arduous. He deserved perhaps a little more leisure. But then again, *le Golf de Barthe* was like his child. To leave all this, he gestured towards the greens, the lakes and the fairway, would be very difficult. He sighed. If he ever came to selling, he would have to find the new owner agreeable. Hugh listened and sympathised and the next summer put a tentative proposal. M. Bernard was interested. Naturally he wanted time to think about it, but...Hugh might perhaps have first refusal. Not immediately, of course. He was not quite ready to retire. This was exactly the kind of arrangement that Hugh wanted as Guy had yet to finish his A-levels.

Three years ago, on the first day of January, M. Bernard finally took his retirement and Hugh and Sally became the proud owners of a golf course. While Sally finished working out her notice in York, Hugh set off for France. It was the wettest spring on record. Hugh phoned us in London to tell us about the mother duck and seven ducklings swimming happily at that moment on one of the greens. Another of M. Bernard's legacies were three elderly geese in permanent residence. They still expect to be fed daily but somehow never seem to get in the golfers' way. The gander even comes into the bar from time to time and demands a drink.

Another odd arrangement came to light a few weeks after Hugh had arrived. A battered old car drew up and a large, weatherbeaten woman carrying something heavy, wrapped in a cloth, marched into the clubhouse. With a cheery *'Bonjour Monsieur,'* she dumped her burden on the bar and turned to go. Hugh, unwrapping it to find a huge, barely plucked turkey complete with head and neck feathers, expressed surprise. She explained cheerfully that this was the customary arrangement with M. Bernard for the use of the small strip of land, which her husband cultivated between the eighth tee and the road. Hugh had been vaguely aware of a few rows of maize or sunflowers in the distance when he had been playing but had hardly had time to pay it much attention. Not having a freezer, he persuaded her to take the bird back, but ever since that day she has proved a good source of corn-fed chicken.

It was the first summer that the *Golf de Barthe* opened under its new ownership that Thomas arrived by himself. His solo week passed quickly and, the tree felled and the fête over, his younger brother Elliot and his parents were due any minute. We went shopping for bedside tables as, yet again, we were rearranging beds in the boys' room. It seemed a long time since we had first borrowed a cot from Claudette to sleep a six-month-old Thomas. The cot that had once long ago been used to sleep, in their turn, both Philippe and Véronique and had been carefully stored up in the *grenier,* for the next generation. Some five summers later, when our second grandchild, baby Elliot arrived, a sturdy wooden cot made by Jean-Michel for Océane was brought up to Bel-Air and reassembled.

For the past few years the boys had managed to share a very large double bed. On their most recent visit, however, the early morning silence, which was normally only broken by the calling of hens before the sound of the church bell floated up from the village at seven, had been disturbed by muffled, but increasingly tense, disputes. This year, to avoid these, we had installed single beds in their room – as far apart as possible. Elliot unpacked his rucksack onto his table and looked approvingly at his bed. But early the next morning after a tentative tap on our bedroom door, it opened with a creak and a small frowning person appeared.

'I just can't keep quiet any longer, Grandma,' came an anguished whisper. 'And I'm not allowed to speak even a single word in there 'cos Thomas is still asleep!' He climbed into our bed, arranged himself between us and we listened perforce in sleepy delight to thousands of words in an ever-ascending treble.

Naturally, the boys couldn't wait to see Hugh and Sally's new golfing venture. We had been once with Raymond and Claudette on a Sunday after-lunch excursion and already the clubhouse had been transformed. There was a smart new bar and french doors now opened onto the refurbished terrace, bright with pots of flowers. But Raymond had been very sceptical. He had never actually met anyone who played golf.

'*Ce n'est pas très connu dans notre region,*' he said dolefully, shaking his head. Clearly, to him, the idea of putting what had presumably been good farming land to such unproductive use was incomprehensible. He was agreeably surprised and eventually, on a second visit, changed his mind when he saw the course and the way the land was being looked after, and especially when he noted that among the English, Dutch, and American players, there were also many French men and women, kitted out as always in the very latest and most elegant gear.

Thomas and Elliot were also impressed, especially when they were taken on a tour of the whole course by buggy, Elliot almost falling out of his seat with excitement at the unexpected ups and downs. Returned at last to the clubhouse, they sat on high stools in the bar and drank Pepsi while Jan, Hugh's new assistant, drew rabbits on Elliot's legs. This was done, he explained to Elliot, to the little French children taken on summer camp, to make sure that they took their evening shower. At any other time Elliot would have protested but he was so overcome by the whole ambience he just giggled. He and Thomas couldn't wait to have a go at golf. They borrowed clubs and went off with their father to practise shots on the driving range. Next, Caz took them round the putting green. That was it; they were hooked!

Back at Bel-Air the usual games of *boules* were forgotten. Frisbies, footballs and badminton racquets were left untouched in the cupboard. All next day they worked designing a golf course. Stones, pine needles, branches and heaps of cut grass were collected to construct bunkers. Their course, they decided, was to have five holes. Unable to dig actual holes in the sun-baked grass, though they did try, they made open-sided rings with small stones. I was coopted to cut up strips of cloth, which they numbered and stapled onto sticks to mark out their putting green, already under construction on the other side of the house. Thomas designed a brochure with a list of charges.

GOLF DE BEL-AIR
2 Francs a round
3 Francs with caddy

The caddy was, of course, Elliot, who was just about tall enough to drag round the bag of croquet mallets, the nearest they could get to golf clubs. All day the game continued and next morning, all disputes forgotten, they were both up and out well before the seven o'clock bell, trimming their greens with scissors. During their two weeks' stay their enthusiasm inevitably waned a little – swimming competitions becoming a counter-attraction – but Thomas was particularly keen and announced his intention of taking up golf when he returned to England.

Other guests came to share in the fun. My goddaughter Joanna and her sister Miranda are old hands at Bel-Air. Daughters of our dear friends, Judith and Barry Foster, *les Fostaires,* as Raymond and Claudette always called them, the girls had first come to Bel-Air as young teenagers, with their brother Jason. While Barry had to return for filming during that long ago summer, Judith and the children had stayed on with us and we had all been initiated into the harvesting of yet another crop, the tobacco.

I remember Grandma, after the large plants were cut and brought to the especially tall barn where they were to dry, showing us how to upend and grasp the heavy sheaves. We had to take great care not to bruise the large, delicate leaves, as we pushed hooks through the tough stems to attach them in fours to wires strung in a line. We then watched as Raymond hoisted each group higher and higher until they disappeared far above our heads, merging into the leafy green canopy above. When all the sheaves were safely suspended and left to dry we, with aching fingers and stiff necks, all returned to the farm and as usual ate *en famille,* the youngsters enjoying each other's company, Philippe especially intrigued by these two budding English beauties. Raymond no longer grows tobacco and the barn is now used for storing the great round *boules* of straw and hay which have replaced the smaller square bales that we also used to arrange by hand.

We are happy that the girls still come back to Bel-Air and now bring their partners and their little boys, Louis and Abie. Raymond is always especially pleased to see them and takes them down to show them the farm. The young families usually spend a few days with us, taking advantage of cheaper mid-week flights before they move into a nearby *gîte*. This time poor Abie arrived white-faced and car-sick.

'Oh, come on in,' said Elliot loftily. 'You'll soon be all right here.'

Abie rapidly recovered but he was, as usual, disappointed not to find a small tent set up in the garden with a tousle-headed girl called Rachel inside. The first summer that Abie could remember coming to Bel-Air, Colin Slee, the then Provost – now renamed Dean of Southwark Cathedral – had come to spend a few days with us. Abie had been so impressed with his daughter Rachel, soon off to read Chinese at university, he had never forgotten her. He thought that she went with the territory and each year he hoped she would reappear.

Rachel and Edith, her mother, had that year fulfilled a long-held ambition to cross the Pyrenees from Spain into France on foot. While Colin, with his friend Brother Sam, a Franciscan friar, had made the journey by car, mother and daughter had set off from the Ordesa National Park. They had spent the night high on the Spanish side watching a shepherd and his dogs far below, while being watched in their turn from above by a huge, native, resident billy-goat. After crossing a glacier they had made their way through the *Brèche de Roland* to Gavranie, where they had rejoined Colin and Sam. We had much enjoyed their company for a few hectic days with romps in the pool and alfresco suppers. Brother Sam, wrapped in a large apron over his shorts, spent all one afternoon carefully preparing a delicious *Boeuf Bourgignon*.

Raymond was very impressed with *Frère* Sam, especially when he and Edith spent some hours helping him with harvesting prunes. As he could neither understand nor translate 'Dean' or 'Provost', he solved that problem by elevating Colin to a Bishop. It is *'l'Évêque* Colin' that he still enquires about from time to time. He was at first slightly over-awed by Colin, who is extremely tall. However, on their last night we all went to another local village celebration and he saw his 'Bishop' dancing wildly with Rachel, both arms held high. Raymond, who is no mean dancer, decided that he thoroughly approved of *'les Anglicans'*, declaring that they were much more liberated than the clergy of the Church of Rome. The Slees and Brother Sam were perfect guests. They intended to leave very early on the morning following the fête, en route for Bilbao and the Guggenheim. We awoke about nine o'clock and, imagining that they must have overslept, hurried to wake them. But the rooms were empty and the beds stripped. They had packed everything, folded their tent, left us an appreciative note and stolen away without making a sound; a remarkable feat in a house with tiled floors and creaking doors.

Car-sickness over, Abie soon cheered up and he and his parents, Miranda and Jonathan, were especially excited this year as, during the winter, they had found and bought an old stone house about half an hour away from us. The completion date was some weeks away and meanwhile the house was being treated for termites, a scary infestation, which we were concerned to discover is not uncommon in the south-west of France. Over the years we have had the odd wood-munching creature in our beams but they are easy to hear and a good squirt of the right product into the wood soon kills them. The problem, as I understand it, with termites is that their particular invasion is silent, often only discovered when what has appeared to be a solid beam turns out to be completely eaten away inside. A termite inspection is now compulsory when a property is sold and any infestation must be notified, treated and paid for by the vendor. We looked forward to seeing the house that they had clearly fallen in love with. We knew the symptoms.

While young and energetic guests were still in residence we took the opportunity to do something about our drive, which on all sides of the house was discoloured and badly overgrown. We put down quantities of weed-killer, made a visit to the quarry for advice, and at eight o'clock the next morning a lorry arrived with ten tonnes of small pale stones aboard. The children all rushed out to watch as the driver advanced slowly, tipping the trailer gently as he came. In a transformation scene worthy of a pantomime, a wide, pristine pathway unrolled the length of the drive as far as the front porch. Unfortunately, the overhanging ash tree prevented the driver from completing a circular tour.

With a grin and a shrug and *'Je suis désolé, Madame, mais…'* the swarthy, handsome young man raised the angle of the trailer and the other five tonnes simply cascaded into a huge, gleaming heap in front of the porch. We got to work with every available rake and shovel.

'We're Roman slaves!' declared the boys, beginning with enthusiasm, but it wasn't long before they were clocking off for liquid refreshment like modern-day workers. It took us the rest of the day and many barrow loads to complete the job. But it looked really impressive – for this year, at least!

Adam and Caz and our boys decided to stay on for another few days. *Les Fostaires* seniors arrived to join their children in the *gîte* before spending time with us at Bel-Air and we all arranged to meet at Libos market to shop for what had become a regular tradition. There is a market somewhere near us on almost every day of the week, but Thursday market at Libos is the largest in the region. The whole centre of the small town is closed to traffic and filled with stalls, which spread their wares up every side street. The food varies with the season, being mostly grown locally, but you may also buy almost anything from tagine pots from North Africa decorated in vivid colours, to tall grandfather clocks in traditional design; even a small, electric car. Rows of rush-seated chairs and double beds stand next to a trailer containing a brace of squealing pigs. There are swaying tunnels of lurid bath towels with life-size prints of a menacing Bengal tiger or a pouting Marilyn Monroe; awnings of tablecloths in Provencal design. There are baskets of unpainted porcelain seconds from Limoges, bags of pine salt to cure a variety of ailments including *'douleurs générales'* and long rows of gleaming knives to slit an animal's throat. We, of course, go to buy food.

We leave the house as early as possible, without breakfast. While most find it impossible not to linger at the first stalls, one of us heads straight for the *boulangerie* to secure the last almond croissants. Almost a foot long, and costing only about eighty pence, they are stuffed with almond paste and generously coated with well-toasted flaked almonds – a real indulgence. The boys keep an eye out and soon enough they've found Abie and Louis in the eager crowds that come pouring in from every inch of car parking space on each side of town. After spending their money on some highly debated bits of plastic, the boys head for the football table in the central bar, called in this region of rugby enthusiasts 'Le Winger'.

With one adult left to keep an eye on them, the rest of us shop for a grand picnic. How easy it is. In twos and threes we return to the café with spit-roasted quail and chicken, and a kilo of *crevettes rosé,* the succulent, firm prawns which taste so different from those caught in Northern waters. We buy still-warm squares of quiche and pizza, helpings of *paella,* ten kinds of olives, great bunches of radishes and basil to put on the huge, field tomatoes. Perhaps we choose a few thin slices of *jambon de pays* to go with the scented melons, the white and yellow peaches, or local *saucisson.* And after making sure that someone has remembered the salad, the milk and the bread we go to choose cheeses, ripe and ready. *Bleu des Causses* perhaps, cheaper than Roquefort and just as good, then a local *Brie,* and for those who prefer a strong, hard cheese, *Bocardo au poivre,* also made in the region.

And then that summer it was, as usual, back through glorious countryside to Bel-Air. While Elliot insisted on demonstrating to Abie his three frantic widths without arm-bands, we set up a table under the ash tree and Raymond soon stopped his tractor to join us for a lengthy aperitif. We imagined Claudette looking at the clock and we waited for her remonstrating phone call. Lunch went on most of the afternoon followed by snoozing in relays, swimming and just enjoying each other's company. Organising everyone, including all the grandchildren, for a group photograph seemed almost more trouble than it was worth, but it was to prove a poignant record of an idyllic day for, the following February, Barry died very suddenly. He was playing in *Art* at the Whitehall Theatre in a part he much enjoyed and his death was a dreadful shock to the cast, his family and his many friends. We have to be thankful that for him there was no lingering illness or diminishing of his formidable power as an actor. Some of his ashes are now buried in the garden of Miranda and Jonathan's lovely house in France. He was a very special, immensely generous, shining comet of a friend and we will never forget him.

We must now make the bed and put flowers in the green room. The umbrella is still there but we hope it won't rain. Our younger son Matthew will be the first to arrive. It will be good to have him here, he is so much of a part of our finding and buying Bel-Air. Later on Judith will come, alas alone, to spend time with us before joining her children. And we will all meet in the market.

CHAPTER EIGHT

In the days before our first guests were due to arrive I spent much of my time in the garden. Up before eight to catch the cool of the morning and busy with the strimmer, the pampas tidied at last, it was beginning to look as though someone lived at Bel-Air. While Mike felt strong enough to cut the grass, I tackled the brambles and the great number of ever-optimistic small suckers from the *sumach* trees. Grandma planted my first *sumach*. Although I am quite happy that the original one has now increased to half a dozen, as they are glorious in early autumn; left to their own devices, they would soon take over the entire garden.

In the market I had bought twenty-five Euro's worth of bedding plants from the lean, brown nurseryman whose soft moustache and black felt hat makes him look like a South American. As he tenderly rolls the petunias, French marigolds, Busy Lizzies and portulaccas in newspaper, he always slips in a few extra plants. This time, he also handed me a small, rather frail looking plumbago. *'Il faut bien la soigner,'* he smiled. 'Look after it well.' If it survived, I thought, it would be yet another plant for Claudette to look after when we left.

Later, the whine of the strimmer happily silenced, at least for that day, I could prepare my tubs and make an instant garden – always a satisfying job. I hoisted each tub up onto the wheelbarrow in order not to have to bend. When I pull my back, as I seem to do almost every summer while working in the garden, I *do* listen when friends advise me to get a gardener. But, apart from the expense, and the fact that I don't really care for over-neat gardens, on a day like this, with the sweet breeze blowing gently from the north and a cloudless sky, I have no intention of sharing this pleasure with anyone. And, if I do hurt my boring back I can visit Dr Frechet, the strong and skilful chiropractor in Agen, who always puts his finger right on the spot and deals with it.

By lunchtime it was too hot to work. We opened the wine, enjoyed a salad and sat gazing at the view. This landscape just seems to soothe the soul. How badly we had needed it. Since these two hours are sacred to both eating and repose there was not even the sound of a distant tractor. The only activity I could see on the brow of the hill was the arching silver spout from my neighbour's water cannon turning silently in a slow, relentless rhythm, the spray catching the sunlight. There was only the whirring of crickets, the warm droning of bees and, higher up from the wood, the occasional staccato burst from a woodpecker.

Later that afternoon we went to visit our friend Simone in hospital. She had broken her leg and was not very happy being incarcerated in a small room on this glorious summer's day. We first heard of Simone, or Mademoiselle L. as we then addressed her, from Portugese Maria, one of Raymond's seasonal workers who came to help with the plum harvest. Maria was slim and very pretty, and as she picked up the large violet plums under the canopy of trees, would talk proudly to us about her Mademoiselle, for whom she normally worked several mornings a week.

'I have told her about you,' she would say. 'She would like so much to meet you. She loves to talk English.' The next time we met she would continue. 'Mademoiselle is really hoping you will call. The house is very easy to find,' she would urge. At that time as well as helping Raymond and Claudette with the plum harvest we were very preoccupied with working on the house and garden, and I'm afraid that speaking English was not very high on our list of priorities. We felt a little guilty but somehow we never got round to paying Mlle L. a visit.

One Sunday afternoon of the following summer we were on a joint wine-tasting expedition somewhere deep in the wooded hillsides of the Lot valley when Raymond, suddenly looking at his watch, announced that we must soon start for home. Mlle L., he informed us, was coming to call. At the time Mike was far more interested in finding another case of really good Cahors, but clearly Raymond felt the impending visit something of a privilege. We drove home along the great curving river valley back to the farm. There, waiting to meet us was a small, neat, bespectacled woman in her sixties whose English needed no practising, being precise, idiomatic and faultless. She clearly loved to talk. She amused us by recounting that in 1951 on her arrival in Scotland as a very young student of English, she had been completely nonplussed by her host shouting at his dog 'Git oot ma hoose!'

Allocated for two days a week as a student teacher in a school in Kirkaldy and thinking she might have time to explore the countryside, she had brought her bicycle all the way from south-west France. But in her spartan lodgings there was nowhere to keep it except in her bedroom and in fact during her whole stay she found the weather so cold and windy that she never took it out.

'I was not awfully happy,' she said. 'There was no

culture on a Sunday, sweets were rationed and I only got one egg a week. And I think my English was worse when I came back that June. But,' she brightened, 'I hitch-hiked alone all over Scotland and thought nothing of it.'

Simone's friendship has brought an extra dimension to our time in France. She lives alone in her family home, a large house with a very interesting garden running down to the river. Although retired she is a formidable scholar with an extensive and eclectic library and our French vocabulary is constantly improved from its inevitably limited and somewhat agricultural bias. She is an avid reader, re-reading all the English classics but also keeping up with current writers. She much enjoyed Barbara Kingsolver's *The Poisonwood Bible* but confessed that she had finally given up on Zadie Smith's *White Teeth!* She also enjoys watching videos, one of her favourites being *Yes Minister.*

She taught for two years in America, in Colorado and California, but most of her working life was spent teaching in Africa. She began in Benin, hardly four years after Independence. On one of her first free weeks, intrepid as ever, she set off with her camera and one companion. In a small car, on bad roads and never sure of finding petrol, they completed 3,000 kilometres in seven days. She took pictures of giraffes and of bands of nomadic Tuaregs with their camels. The women wore enormously heavy copper bracelets on their ankles, which were for sale, and they would offer to go to the blacksmith to have them removed with a hammer. Simone bought several which she later used for paperweights. From the banks of the Niger she watched children swimming eagerly to school, their clothes and books neatly packaged on their heads.

For thirteen years she taught in a college in Togo, which eventually became a university. The people and their culture began to fascinate her. She now has a wonderful collection of carvings, exotic combs, highly decorated masks and small and intricate Ashanti gold weights. We love to call on her after market and sip an aperitif for there is always something fascinating to see or to hear. She described to us how during her time in Togo she would examine the artefacts the travelling pedlars brought her, never knowing what she would find. They soon got to appreciate her real interest in African art. As they unwrapped their tattered bundles, and spread out their wares, she gradually became a connoisseur and it was her delight to discover something really old and of great beauty.

She had been amused when we told her of our grandson's new passion for golf. She had herself been a keen golfer. She described the golf courses she played on in Africa, not the traditional green sward but a course constructed of a mixture of sand made smooth with oil, which was laid out onto the bare earth. Sadly she plays no longer. On her return from Africa some years ago, she was treated for ovarian cancer. It was in the early days of radiotherapy and the dose used was far too strong. The cancer was cured but the damage done to the surrounding nerves at that time has now begun to take its toll. She is becoming increasingly immobile. Now in hospital, she urged us to go to her home where her brother had brought up from the *cave* all her golfing paraphernalia.

'He will be there tomorrow,' she said 'I have told him you will telephone and you are to take it all for Thomas.'

On the way home from the hospital we called into the local DIY store to see if we could find some plain, white, mirrored cupboards for our bathroom, which had been newly refurbished the previous year.

Most of the very gradual improvements that we have made to Bel-Air over twenty-five years have pleased us. The one exception was the bathroom. Of course any bathroom at all was like a miracle in those early days, when we washed in a plastic bowl on a camping table. We later progressed to china basins and jugs but we still fetched our water in buckets from an outside tap, marginally easier than hauling it up from the well, which Anaïs, my predecessor, had always done. Although mains water had arrived at Bel-Air a few years before we bought the house, Anaïs had never had a tap installed. That water was metered, the old lady and her handicapped son had been too poor to pay for it and, of course, water from the well was free. And at that time, we heated our water, as she must also have done, in an iron pot over the fire.

Our first concession to modern convenience had been an outside lavatory. This was closely followed by a kitchen corner built into the main living room, with a large, square, white china sink and simple pine cupboards made by a local craftsman. We were still in the very early stages of restoring the house when we finally saved enough money for the bathroom. What to choose? I was very concerned to *conserver le style* of the old house and reluctant to change what I still saw as its romantically derelict state. I was besotted with the rough thick walls, the hand-hewn granite sink in the earth-floored corridor, the window opening with its nail-studded wooden shutter, the great gnarled oak beams. It was almost hesitantly that we stripped the old varnish from Anaïs's tall, cherry-wood side-board with the carved board at the base, and gently peeled off the dirty oil-cloth which had been stuck onto the long pine table.

During those first winter months back in London, we searched in junk shops for old lamps, candlesticks, marble topped wash-stands, pine chests and towel rails and more flowered china jugs and basins; all, of course much cheaper then than now. Friends would give us the odd plate or rug, which they thought might just do at Bel-Air. A definite 'look', a sort of faded early-Victorian rustic, seemed to be the most appropriate. But a bathroom was difficult to plan. A self-conscious Victorian reproduction would have looked odd and been far too expensive and, in the end, we settled for the most simple white bath, bidet, and a basin set in a pine surround. But how to finish the walls and floor? We were very happy with the large, traditional, terracotta floor tiles which M. Carnejac had laid in the main room, and I made the mistake of choosing for the bathroom tiles in a similar colour, albeit smaller and roughly glazed.

At first the sheer pleasure of a bathroom, any bathroom, was sufficient delight. Wallowing in hot water after strenuous days up ladders, painting walls, wrestling with the garden, or harvesting straw bales, potatoes, plums or tobacco, was the ultimate luxury, especially with a generous aperitif! It was only after many years and looking at other bathrooms that I had to admit that I had made a stupid mistake. Our bathroom was undeniably gloomy. Even though it faced south and the fierce sunlight, the window was very small and high. The dark red tiles I had chosen so long ago were just wrong.

M. Carnejac's tiling was, of course, immaculate. How could we possibly think of destroying it? He had even tiled the small square space that had been cut into the wall beneath where the stairs had once ascended, rickety and uneven, to the attic. According to Raymond, in every old house there had always been a hiding place for gold sovereigns, *les Louis d'or*, cut in the staircase wall. Alas, we found nothing in ours but dead spiders.

I wondered if it might be possible to paint over the tiles. But if the paint began to peel it would look even worse. We were slightly embarrassed when, eventually, we explained to M. Carnejac that, beautiful though his tiling undoubtedly was, we finally wished to change it. We had simply chosen the wrong colour. He agreed.

'*Mais, ne vous inquiétez pas.* Don't worry,' he said. '*Pas de problème,*' his favourite phrase. 'Just choose something lighter.' He had already unfolded his *mètre pliant* and was beginning to measure. 'It won't take long. I shall retile over the top.'

'I didn't realise that was a possibility,' I said with relief, having had visions of hours of hammering, shattered tiles and clouds of dust.

He smiled. '*Bien sûr!* And, I can tell you,' he added, 'it will be much easier than it was the first time round. These old walls were so uneven. Now I've got a good strong surface. Just choose tiles of a different size.'

Off we went to buy large, gleaming white wall tiles and, to add just a touch of colour, a narrow tile in an acid yellow to make a thin line running all round the room, one tile from the top. We chose a larger, dull white tile for the floor and, while we were at it, a new basin and bidet. M. Carnejac and M. Fernandez, the plumber, exchanged greetings and promised that it would all be done by the following spring. We have found that local craftsmen are quite glad to have work on the back-burner to tide them over the winter months. Sometimes a judicious phonecall about a month before our intended arrival is a good idea, and during that winter when I phoned Raymond he told me that he had just bumped into M. Fernandez in the market and reminded him.

When we returned the following spring we were extremely pleased with our new bathroom, and amazed at the difference made by white tiles. Now all that remained was to find two plain white cupboards with mirrored doors. This was proving to be the most difficult task and we had already rejected every single model in the more upmarket bathroom shops. The French have a penchant for mirrored cupboards, but neither the mirrors nor the cupboards must on any account be plain. Large, Art Deco sheaves of lilies are fashionable as are gliding swans, ladies dressed like Madame de Pompadour or galleons in full sail. Even the plainest mirrors have delicately etched borders. Eventually it was in the definitely downmarket DIY section of a hypermarket that we found what we were looking for. The cupboards were white, well-made and, above all, plain, and the next day we fixed them safely to the wall.

In three days' time we would go to collect our younger son, Matthew, from Agen. He was part of the stage crew on the new West End musical *'Bombay Dreams'* and could only manage a week with us. His brother and the rest of the family would join him on the following day and, we hoped, stay longer. In any case, Bel-Air would soon be *complet*. Matthew always preferred to sleep in our fourth bedroom, which we had made in the *chai*. We called it the green room, not in any theatrical sense, but because many years before in a wild spasm of decorating we had stencilled twining green leaves the length of a painted beam and even, for good measure, trailed a few more leaves up the wall behind the bed. Although the walls and floor were white, the room gradually acquired green bedcovers and rugs and the odd green and white plate adorned the walls. As I dusted, removing the latest spiders' webs, and squeezed the lavender bags, which hang from the beam, I prayed that we would not get any heavy rain, as we still had done nothing about roofing over the corner of the house directly outside the green room door. The heap of old tiles that the boys had uncovered kept reminding us.

Early that evening Jean-Michel came by to catch a cow that was calling forlornly from the edge of the vineyard. There always seems to be one young animal more curious than the rest that will eventually push its way under the electric fence and wander off. When the herd move on and it suddenly finds itself separated from the others, it becomes worried. We could hear the older cow, which acts as 'mother' to the nine or ten young ones, answering, but it was clear that Jean-Michel would have to switch off the current and lead the young cow back. He climbed down from the tractor and, baton in hand, strode up through the long, lush grass. There was quite a chorus from the cows as they saw him and we heard him calling soothingly as he approached *'Bene, bene.'* Cows hereabouts must be called in the old language, Occitan, which Grandma and Grandpa still often used when they chatted to each other.

The young cow rescued, Jean-Michel appeared round the side of the house. *'Le bar est ouvert?'* he demanded with a grin.

'Bien sur!'

Looking bronzed and fit he took a beer from the fridge, and sat down, taking off his orange baseball cap, which was stained with sweat. Although he is very dark-skinned his deep-set eyes are an amazing blue. He and Véronique, with Océane, had been to Cap d'Agde the previous weekend. Véronique has a job in Villeneuve, at Auchan, the hypermarket. She works shifts, sometimes not getting home until after ten at night. They both work extremely hard but also enjoy themselves in ways that to previous generations would have been inconceivable. They think nothing of driving for three hours through a Saturday night down to the Mediterranean to spend Sunday with friends and relations in their tiny apartment overlooking the busy harbour, only to drive home again in the early hours of Monday morning. Raymond mutters about farmers not expecting to be free at the weekend and what Grandpa would have said had he, Raymond, suggested such a thing, but as long as he is fit to keep an eye on the animals the youngsters will take an occasional break.

'There's rain forecast for tomorrow and the day after,' said Jean-Michel, draining his beer. We grimaced. 'We've got Matthew coming to stay in the green room and we've still done nothing about getting that corner roofed over. It's not much fun having to go out in the rain to the bathroom.'

Jean-Michel laughed. *'Matthieu? Il est solide lui.* A bit of rain won't bother him!'

'Perhaps not, but we've got others less *solide* coming in a few weeks. It's getting someone to do it – even if it's possible. Raymond says old M. Lecours has retired.'

'C'est vrai. And in any case he was always more interested in his pigeon shooting than his roofs. You should have a word with M. Carpentier,' urged Jean-Michel. 'He's been helping me during the winter. He and his son are good workers. And he's reasonable too, especially if you pay *en liquide,'* he grinned,

rubbing thumb and forefingers together.

We hadn't even considered M. Carpentier. He was a near neighbour. We had met him and his family at the village fête the previous year but we had imagined that he wouldn't have a minute to spare, so busy was he on his own project.

Until M. Carpentier's recent arrival, nothing has ever been done to an overgrown ruin that lay at the bottom of our track about a hundred yards in from the road. It was the first building we passed on turning into our long, winding *chemin rural* that led down over a stream, climbed between Jean-Michel's house and barn, and curved on up the hill to our house. Although very close to the track, the old ruin always seemed withdrawn, being an L-shape with the long windowless side of a barn abutting directly onto the track and the shorter section of the house hidden from view. It belonged, we learnt, to M. Guyou, whose own farm lay in the dip between two nearby fields where his large herd of black and white milking cows moved leisurely over the horizon at regular intervals. While he stored great rounds of straw in the barn, he did nothing to maintain it. The house, completely abandoned, became almost entirely obscured by wild plum trees and brambles. Gradually the roof began to deteriorate and one spring when we arrived, we saw that the corner of the barn wall had collapsed.

Raymond shrugged. *'C'est dommage,'* he said,

'*mais*...he won't spend the money. They do say he'd like to sell it but...' he shook his head. '*C'est trop près du chemin.*' It's too near the track. That summer we did have an unexpected visit from a lost English couple clutching a map and an estate agent's leaflet. When they realised that the house they were looking for was the ruin they had driven past without a glance, they soon disappeared. M. Guyou, it seemed, was over-optimistic.

However, the following year when we arrived we were surprised to see that all the brambles had been cleared, the house was visible, and stakes now marked out a large piece of land on three sides of the property. A gravel path had even been laid. We were curious.

'*Oui, c'est vendu,*' said Raymond at supper that night as we caught up with all the news. '*Aux Anglais?*' we asked.

'*Non, c'est un M. Carpentier qui l'a achetée.*' He then explained that M. Carpentier and his family had been renting a small house not far away. 'He's had his eye on it for ages,' said Raymond. 'Waiting for the price to come down, or the roof to fall in completely.'

'Or both,' laughed Claudette.

'*Oui,*' Raymond agreed. '*Mais, il est maçon.* He's a builder and so is his son. *Ils sont gentils tous les deux.*'

As we drove by we caught glimpses of a dark, handsome man, but the work on the house seemed to be very spasmodic. More obvious was the beginning of a garden on which Madame Carpentier soon began to make an impression. We learnt that both her husband and her son were employed by a large, building company and, as a consequence, work on their own project could only be done at weekends and in their holidays. However, by the next time we came it was clear that M. Carpentier had ambitious plans for the once derelict building. A large picture window had been cut, and a covered terrace built, the roof supported on slender, very white, columns. This Grecian effect was not universally approved of locally where traditional designs are favoured and there were mutterings in the village shop, but he was clearly a skilful builder.

Jean-Michel drained his beer. '*Merci*,' he said, picking up his cap and striding off again. 'Il *faut parler à Monsieur Carpentier, Michel*,' he shouted over the roar of the tractor. And so we did.

The following evening M. Carpentier came up to look at our problem. 'Mm,' he frowned. '*C'est pas facile*.' We rather suspected that to be the case. The two roof edges, which needed to be joined to make a porch, sloped at right angles to each other. M. Carpentier explained, however, as he and Mike drew endless diagrams, that that was not the main problem. He nailed a string to the highest point between the two sloping roofs and pulled it out on a diagonal. We began to see that what was needed was a stout wooden upright at the far corner, to support a diagonal beam. What was in effect a rectangle could be divided and incorporated into the other two roof edges. The larger problem was the height, or rather lack of height, as both roofs sloped down very low.

'The covered terrace would be perfectly accessible from the bedroom door,' said M. Carpentier. 'People would not get wet when they came out to the shower, but,' he frowned. 'Because the ground is higher out here, if you roof it over, no one will be able to get into the shower room or the lavatory from outside without bending very low.'

Bending low not being recommended for problem backs, it was clear that we would have to think again. M. Carpentier scratched his head.

'What I could do,' he said, pacing about and squinting up at the roof, 'is dig the ground out further back to here.'

'What about the water channel?' Our water channel, which M. Duparq had made all round the house many years before, only just managed to cope with the great volume of water that cascaded down from the long slope of the roof of the *chai* during heavy rain.

'I'll cut some steps going down so that you won't bump your head,' said M. Carpentier, 'and then create a new channel for the water. A drain and a perforated pipe under the drive here will carry the water right away.'

It made sense.

'And, the upright,' we hesitated. 'It will be of wood?'

He grinned, realising that we had his Grecian columns in mind.

'*Oh oui. Ne vous inquiétez pas. Très rustique!*'

'When could you start?' we asked hopefully after he had quoted us a price – *en liquide* of course – which seemed reasonable. He looked apologetic.

'I can't even begin to think about it. Not until the middle of September,' he said with a shrug. '*Désolé, mais...*'

It looked as though the heap of tiles would stay where they were for a while yet, and the umbrella remain at the ready by the green room door.

Chapter Nine

Although rain was forecast Jean-Michel was taking no chances. I was awoken the next morning by the swish of the water cannon. During the night it had been working its way up the great field of maize just behind Bel-Air, which seemed to grow taller every day. As the jet completed its final sweeping arcs before winding itself back onto the revolving drum to stop, I knew that the spray would just reach my garden. Pleased at the prospect of a free *arrosage,* I nevertheless got up to close the shutters. The hissing water grew louder each time it turned towards the house and soon the first heavy splashes sounded on my bedroom door. When the cannon is not in use I am still able to get free water by attaching my garden hose to Raymond's hydrant at the corner of the orchard. This new system brings water to all the surrounding farms from the river Lot.

It smells strongly of river, but is much cheaper for the farmers than using mains water. Raymond is generous and claims that even if I put my sprinkler on all the afternoon, it is just a dribble compared to his *canon à eau*. I don't argue.

He had reminded me the previous evening that it was the *fête votive* at St Aubin the following day. Later in the year, on the second Sunday in September, the celebrated *Foire aux Pruneaux* would be held in this small village about six kilometres away and would attract about four thousand visitors. The main winding street would be arched over with paper garlands made during the winter months and in this region of plum orchards people would come from all over Lot-et-Garonne to taste and buy prunes, *les pruneaux d'Agen,* presented in every conceivable way. There would be prunes in tarts, in cakes, covered in chocolate, cooked on skewers with bacon, *en daube de boeuf,* or steeped in an almost lethal *Eau de Vie* – also distilled from prunes! The Bishop of Agen would come to say a special Mass in Occitan and to bless a tray of the most beautiful prunes presented by small girls in local costume. There would be folkdancing and donkey rides.

Today's fête would be a much smaller affair but Raymond was exhibiting the old Citroën, and hoped we would go. We arrived in time to see him, dressed in a striped jersey and peaked cap, posing proudly with other owners for a group photograph. Our Citroën stood between a 1929 Ford Cabriolet and another Citroën, 1936 vintage, called 'Rosalie'. The cars gleamed from every surface. The photographic session complete, Raymond began to enquire about the menu *pour le repas de midi*.

'They give you lunch?' I asked.

'*Naturellement*,' said Raymond. *'On n'exhibite pas pour rien!'* Now I began to understand another reason for his enthusiasm for *Le Club des Vieilles Voitures*.

The cars looked positively modern compared with another exhibit; a really ancient, wooden threshing machine, which was being coupled to an old tractor. A group of sturdy young enthusiasts rushed about with sheaves of wheat. When three brand new hessian sacks were hooked onto one side of the thresher to catch the grain, I realised that I hadn't seen a hessian sack for years. Although plastic sacks would not have been appropriate, these, although made of natural fibre, were so pristine they also looked incongruous hanging against the well-worn, battered wooden machine, as though a careless property master had forgotten to age the props. As the machine began to shudder into life, sending up great clouds of dust, it looked as though it might fall to pieces at any minute. More sheaves were brought. The sacks began to fill with grain, the oldest watchers in the crowd smiled with pleasure and turned to tell of how their fathers had known such a machine.

There was much talk of *les beaux jours d'autrefois,* 'the good old days', but after the machine had broken down for the third time the crowd drifted away to watch a game of *rampeau* being played nearby.

I am told that this game predates *pétanque,* which, in any case, originates from south-east France. A simple, local game, it is similar to skittles and is played on a bed of sand about four metres long and a metre wide, with a board for a back-stop. The skittles, or *quilles,* are very thin wooden pegs, and are placed one behind the other in the sand about forty centimetres apart. The ball is also made of wood. As we watched one attempt after another it appeared much more difficult to down all three pins than one would have imagined. After each throw the pins were straightened and the sandy channel was solemnly reshaped using a curious kind of wooden implement – a half-circle on a long handle. The curved underneath edge smoothed the channel along which the ball had to be rolled. We had, many years before, found just such a tool in our attic and could not imagine what it had been used for until we saw our first game played, also at a local fête. We wondered then whether, long before Anaïs married and came to Bel-Air, her husband Justin and his two young brothers had once played *rampeau* in our garden.

Part of the fun of the game is the thwack of the ball against the wooden board, in this case an old door lain on its side. At each attempt there were shouts of approval if two pins fell, commiseration at near misses.

'Deux sur trois! Pas mauvais Jean-Claude,' is the shout. Others step forward to try, but no one manages to down all three. When the ball misses altogether and slams into the door there are jeers and ironic 'Bravos.' The keeper has a satisfied gleam in his eye as he comes forward yet again to rake the sand. I begin to wonder if the final pin is more firmly fixed than perhaps is permissible until the little crowd stands back to allow someone who, from the whispers, might be a champion to try his luck. He is a short, solid, unsmiling man. Under his brand new flat cap, each section cut from a differently patterned fabric, his eyes narrow. He takes the ball and shuffles it from hand to hand. The crowd grow restless then quieten as he squints, bends his knees. His arm flashes back, the ball is hurled with great force and all the pins fly out of the sand.

'Trois, sur trois!' they yell in delight to the hero of the hour and crowd round to congratulate him. He permits himself a brief smile, adjusts his cap and strides away. The keeper rakes the bowling channel anew but there are no challengers.

The next morning there were 25 swallows on the electricity wire, the air was definitely cooler and banks of cloud moved slowly toward us from the west. From the orchard I could hear much shouting of explanations by Jean-Michel over the roar of the tractor, but as there was no loud, protesting response, I thought it unlikely to be Raymond working with him. It was, unusually, Philippe, unshaven and wearing what looked like his father's straw hat, who greeted me. He was driving the tractor with a great round bale of straw balanced on the *fourche* in front. Jean-Michel, with customary aplomb, was showing him how to lower the bale into a small trailer, fitted with a rotating disc. This sliced up the bale and spewed the straw out at the side like a motor mower. When they had coordinated their efforts, Jean-Michel drove up and down between the rows of plum trees, covering the ground with straw.

'It will stop the plums bursting when they fall on the hard ground, or getting muddy when it rains,' he told me. It was the first time I had ever seen this done and was clearly another of Jean-Michel's new ideas and probably why Philippe, rather than Raymond, was involved. Philippe, who lives in Toulouse, works for a sugar company, but most weekends during the summer, he and Corinne with young Clement return to the countryside where Philippe keeps a hunting dog. He is a very good shot and also enjoys fishing. The young couple divide their time between their parents' farms, returning to the city late on a Sunday evening with enough fresh produce to last until the following weekend.

I left them hard at work, took my breakfast and sat by the pool. Two swallows were now dive-bombing the bubble plastic cover, which we pull over at night to maintain the water temperature. After I rolled it back, a third swallow joined them and they entertained me with spectacular whirling and diving to take small sips from the surface of the pool at speed. They then flew up to preen themselves on the wire, showing their pale underbellies with just a hint of darker blue. Suddenly there was a flurry and the wire was bare. A squadron of birds took off, swooping and diving close to the water. The whole formation rose, turned restlessly, now skimming over the maize, now flying low over the house, always returning eventually, to sit like a row of thick dark commas along the length of the wire.

This unusually early display presaged a sudden and very real change in the weather. The sun made a last, brief appearance during the afternoon but that night the temperature dropped dramatically and for the next few days the rain was continuous. This dire and unseasonal weather was apparently all over Europe, reaching as far as Russia. That evening we lit the fire in the wide *cheminée* and, as we watched the water cascading off our roof and pouring down the water channel round the house, we heard on the radio that the rain in London was so heavy that even some underground stations were closed. And the following day, still it rained.

It was our village fête at the weekend. It looked like being a very damp affair. Mike's convalescence was sufficient excuse for us not to attend, but Raymond, indefatigable as ever, was busy trying to work out how he could combine going to the fête with attending a golden wedding on the same day. Rico, Claudette's cousin, the *ancien mécanicien* who had restored the old Citroën, was celebrating with his jolly wife. Raymond felt obliged to go and, of course, the menu was sure to be special.

'*On a commencé avec un apéritif et des amuses-gueules,*' Raymond began next day as he gave us a report, his eyes shining. The aperitif was a *pousse rapier,* guaranteed to get any party going. This is a Gascon aperitif, named, it is suggested, after D'Artagnan, who was pretty handy with a *rapier.* The aperitif is often served in a special glass with a *rapier* drawn on the side, by which the amount of liqueur, an orange-flavoured Armagnac, is measured. This is then topped up with a sparkling white wine, sometimes referred to as *un vin sauvage.* At three o'clock the meal proper had begun with *crudités,* then *foie gras, poelé avec un feuilleté.* Next, said Raymond, they had barbecued a whole lamb, his eyes glazing over as he described its succulence. He did comment briefly on the fruit dessert, but extolled the *pièce montée,* the French version of a wedding cake. This consists of dozens of small round éclairs filled with *crème pâtissière,* glued together with caramel to form as high a concoction as the skill of the chef will allow. The meal was followed by a *grand concours de pétanque*.

Raymond was, apparently, doing very well until, as he explained, he had to drag himself away to be in time for the *repas* at the village fête, which of course he couldn't miss. He then sat down to roast pork, sautée potatoes and haricots, followed by cheese and fruit tart. As Raymond and Claudette and the rest of our not-to-be-defeated village then danced in the rain, we had lain in bed with hot water bottles and listened to the music drifting up across the maize. Perhaps *l'année prochaine* we would be more *en forme*. The weather improved. The sun reappeared, the fields steamed and the orchard was carpeted with great violet plums. As we watched the pickers bending to fill their baskets we realised that Jean-Michel had got the straw down just in time.

The next day we went to collect Matthew. The road from Villeneuve to Agen is treacherous with many dangerous bends. In a real effort to reduce the large number of accidents, the French have recently decided on an imaginative, albeit chilling, strategy. We were startled when we saw our first, life-size, black figure silhouetted against the green hedgerow. By the time we reached Agen we had passed fourteen such macabre cut-outs marking the spot where fatalities had occurred. It is a sobering and, I imagine, much more effective remedy than a simple speed restriction.

Matthew decided that one of his first tasks must be to tackle our much overgrown wisteria. Although, sadly, we had not been here to see it flower, by the number of pods hanging all along its length it had clearly been very beautiful. Now long, looping tendrils had already reached out to encircle the Cyprus tree and, more worrying, were pushing their way up under the roof tiles and winding into a stranglehold round the chimney. It seemed impossible to believe that some years before, I had been worried about losing it altogether. It had endured very rough treatment when we finally decided to have the rendering taken off the south-facing outside wall where it grew.

We had by that time already stripped off much of the old earth rendering inside the house. This was not so much a deliberate choice as the fact that the surface was so loose that each inadvertent knock as a piece of furniture was repositioned resulted in another clod falling to the floor. When, in our bedroom, we finally took a mallet and finished the job, we uncovered very attractive stones, which we then had sandblasted. Re-pointed with cream-coloured cement, they still give us pleasure when we wake up.

Outside the house, however, we had done very little, especially on the south side, which faced the track. The very oldest section with its patched rendering stones just visible here and there, had a certain charm and also, I reasoned, made it less likely that any passing burglar would expect to find anything of value in such an unkempt dwelling. In twenty-five years we have only been burgled once. They were clearly professionals. They simply removed the only object of any real value, a hanging brass lamp. A nearby chateau, which they next visited, was not so fortunate and a great deal of valuable furniture was taken.

Eventually Mike, always more practical, persuaded me that something simply had to be done about the state of this outside wall.

'We must decide either to re-render it completely,' he said, 'or take off all the old *crépi,* and if the stones are good like those inside, we can leave it *pierre apparente.'*

This exterior finish for stone houses has become much more popular but needs to be done skilfully. The cement used to re-point must harmonise with the stones, as if it is too dark it can dominate. Sufficient cement must be used to seal the joins and make the wall waterproof, but, at the same time, the best effect is achieved by leaving the edges of the stones just proud enough to reveal their shape. This is time-consuming. We have watched many builders with varying skills throwing on the very wet cement, pushing it between the stones and then scraping or sometimes brushing it off.

As with most decisions, we left it for yet another

year. It was the burgeoning ivy that finally made us realise that we could wait no longer. Each time we cut it back and pulled away the ever-thickening stems, another chunk of rendering came with it – especially on the oldest section of the wall under the hand-cut window. Large spaces had begun to open up behind the loose *crépi*. Just how large I realised one hot morning in late September as I surprised a long, basking snake. Alarmed at my shadow, she slid her head into what seemed to be a small hole but then completely disappeared, retracting the tip of her tail in a last flick. I worried about what else might make a home in our wall.

We decided then to have all the old *crépi* removed and take a chance on the stones. We telephoned M. Duparq. He came a few days later, listened, nodded and '*Hmmned*' and banged a bit of *crépi* off with his boot.

'*Il me semble que les pierres sont solides et assez jolies,*' he said reassuringly. He would be happy to work at it in October. Before we left we cut down all the honeysuckle round the bedroom door and those branches of the pomegranate which were nearest the wall. I pruned, pulled forward and staked my favourite climber, a *campsis radicans,* called locally a *bignonia.* It has spectacular red trumpet flowers in July and August and can tolerate extremes of temperature. I hoped that M. Duparq would be able to work between it and the wall without too much difficulty. I built a small platform with planks and bricks over my sleeping Madonna lilies, wrote a notice *'Attention!'* and hoped that my garden would survive the onslaught. By Christmas we had received the last of the small, handwritten bills for M. Duparq's careful labour in the autumn sunshine. He hoped we would be pleased.

When we arrived the following spring we were delighted to see that the stones were indeed *jolies,* the pointing sensitively done and all the plants unharmed. But even as we admired our wall we realised that this improvement had created an even greater contrast between the original part of the house and the newer addition. We had grown used to the different roof tiles on the two sections of the house. They no longer bothered us. Unlike the old-style Roman curved tiles on the original part of the house, the 1889 tiles were smaller and flatter but they had weathered attractively, and were watertight. But now, below the roof, the remaining narrow section of solid, greyish cement-rendered wall next to the long wall of newly exposed pale stones, reproached us. What other beautiful stones might lie hidden? If this surface was also made *pierre apparente* the whole back of the house would be in harmony. We had to try it.

M. Duparq returned. He had another job on hand and could only work for us on a Saturday, he told us; not, as he had always previously done, continuing on a Sunday morning. *'C'est ma femme,'* he said solemnly. His wife had apparently put her foot down. The following Saturday he arrived at eight in the morning. We cut back the wisteria, untied it, and he helped me gently lower the great twisting stems to the ground. It looked like some fantastic slumbering creature from an Arthur Rackham drawing. But, in his enthusiasm as he uncovered the – we hoped – attractive stones, would he remember not to step backwards onto the wisteria? How could it avoid being bruised and battered by falling cement? The rendering on this section of the house was a much more modern mixture and consequently heavier and, we feared, more difficult to remove.

M. Duparq set up his scaffold board on two small iron trestles and got to work. He worked for four hours without stopping, then, as always, disappeared at noon. It looked promising. On his return at two o'clock he then continued until about five, when he called us to come and see how good the stones were. He had just reached the window and was satisfied to discover that it was framed in the traditional manner with large, hand-cut stone edging. Below it there was a mixture of larger, square-cut stones and smaller horizontal layers. We were all sure that we had made the right decision. There were even one or two edges of flat red tiles aesthetically placed. We kept looking with pleasure at the half-finished wall during the following week, impatient to see the work completed.

The weather held fine. The following Saturday he arrived as usual and as we worked in the garden on the other side of the house we could hear the tap tap of his hammer. But during the afternoon it suddenly stopped and M. Duparq appeared, covered in dust and looking very worried.

'You'd better come and have a look,' he said.

He had now reached the end section of the wall directly under the chimney and, instead of beautiful stones, had suddenly begun to uncover a jumble of broken bricks, small stones and rubble. None of us had realised that when the new section had been built, the chimney had simply been cut into the wall, unlike the *cheminée* in the old part of the house, which is a separate construction.

'I'll have to just carry on, take it all off and... and see what can be done,' said M. Duparq gloomily. By the end of the afternoon when he had knocked out all the rubble, our otherwise beautiful wall had a savage, soot-blackened wound running from top to bottom, which became even wider as it descended to the actual back of the fireplace. M. Duparq, sweating, stood back. He scratched his head, moving his cotton sunhat back and forth. He lit a small roll-up and just stood and gazed at the wall. Eventually he turned to us. '*Ne vous inquiétez-pas*,' he said. 'Don't worry.' '*Je peux le refaire.*' We knew his skill with stones. He had built our wall by the pool but, as we looked at the jagged sooty edges, the broken lumps of crude red brick, we were not hopeful.

It seemed that M. Duparq had a few days holiday from his regular work for, after spending Sunday with his wife, he returned first thing on Monday morning, a pile of stones rumbling around in the back of his battered truck. 'You can look when it is finished,' he said firmly. Intermittently he trundled about with the wheelbarrow searching for the precise stone he wanted, finding others in the garden or from a ruined wall at the end of the track. We heard him throw down his scaffold board at the halfway mark but left him to it until at the end of the day he called us. It was a triumph. The join was invisible. Even M. Duparq allowed himself a grin of satisfaction at our surprised delight.

'*Pas mal,*' he said. 'Not bad.' He replaced the scaffold. 'I'll come back tomorrow and do the pointing.'

By the time he had finished, the wisteria, which we had all but forgotten in our anxiety about the wall, was badly bruised, bedraggled and covered in cement dust. We hosed it down, pruned off damaged branches and did our best to tie the remnants back up to the wires. As we now watched Matthew wrestling with its enormous growth it was clear that our wisteria was indestructible.

That evening we went into Monflanquin to eat. The annual medieval festival was in full swing. We would miss the final banquet on the following night because we had to go once more to Agen to collect the rest of the family. On previous years the grandchildren had usually managed to coincide their visit with the great spectacle. Mike made them cardboard helmets and shields covered in silver foil, which still hang in their room. I seem to remember once knitting silver chain-mail tops and sewing red crosses onto tabards made out of old sheets. Thomas is now a little too sophisticated to participate but Elliot was annoyed at missing all the fun.

The dishes, from medieval recipes, for the great banquet itself used always to be provided and prepared by a committee of farmers' wives. It was excellent. Now, however, common market regulations have stopped all that enterprise and enthusiasm. Professional caterers must be used for such a large number. *'Ces imbeciles de Bruxelles!'* is the complaint so often voiced here – especially when things to eat are concerned. I noticed when we arrived this summer that a large, butcher's shop-sized cold store was humming away in Claudette's hangar. On enquiring, she told me that this year her precious calf had not gone to the abattoir. Robert had butchered it in situ and her *ris de veau,* her *cervelle* and all the other delicacies had been saved. The French take a real delight in frustrating what they see as unnecessary regulations. I remember the glee when there was, one year, a brief petrol strike.

'Oui, c'est la grève!' declared the postman excitedly as he waved my letters at me from his little yellow van. He, of course, was exempt! It was extremely inconvenient, not least for those holiday-makers who had not filled their tanks in time to get home. Friends of ours who live in France and have imbibed the national attitude, had just left us in their camping van to tour the Gorges du Tarn. They rang to say that they had spent the next week in a field, not far away, walking to the nearby shops and declared it extremely enjoyable and much more relaxing.

Brussels notwithstanding, Monflanquin was *en fête*. Blue and yellow banners hung from every balcony and many of the people strolling the streets were in costume. The air was filled with smoke from the many small barbecues in the square and the appetizing smell of meat cooking with garlic and fresh herbs. I'm not sure what Brussels think about these. Perhaps they are next on the list! Under the lights, stalls were selling trinkets, stone carvings, masks and hand made soaps. Jugglers, fire-eaters and tumblers paraded by. Small boys in tights and jerkins chased each other with wooden swords, little girls in long skirts and aprons sat chatting on the wall, or rode solemnly by on donkeys. Chicken roamed about pecking up bits of fallen food in the straw underfoot.

As we climbed the manure-strewn street a parade of gaudily dressed horsemen came down toward us, their mounts splendid with scarlet caparison and jingling harness. Later in the evening there would be jousting in the square by the church. The leaders with unfurled banners and plumed helmets were grand and imperious but they were followed by a horde of ruffians with blackened teeth, wild hair, bandaged limbs and crutches; their cosmetic wounds and suggestions of the pox almost too realistic. The wenches were authentically dirty with matted locks and greasy costumes. I imagine these are young actors who spend their summers going from one medieval festival to another across France. Some of them are very skilled musicians on authentic instruments and there is always a small group whose speciality seems to be a delight in looking as revolting as possible. They banged their drums and tambours, squeaked their pipes, clattered their sticks, as they capered about and whooped and sang. In the middle of this street of medieval cacophony stood a small tubby Frenchman, immaculate in white shorts, white sports shirt with the neat green crocodile of Lacoste on his left breast, white socks to the knee and spotless shoes. Under one arm he held an equally white poodle on a jewelled lead. In the other hand he held his mobile phone into which he continued to shout as the crowd, heaving and shrieking, surged round him, swallowed him up and then moved on leaving him still remonstrating, and completely oblivious.

CHAPTER TEN

The rest of the family arrived safely. Thomas was highly delighted with his golfing trolley and its contents and was impatient to try them out. When we made our next trip to Hugh and Sally's golf course his boxes of Simone's golf balls, still in their original Jack Nicklaus wrappers were examined with interest by other players, pronounced rare and quite possibly valuable, which pleased him. While he set off to practise, Sally took Elliot to feed the geese and then to the nearest lake which was full of fish and, in spite of a recent visit by yet another of M. Bernard's former cronies, also frogs. One quiet afternoon, Hugh told us, a total stranger had turned up with a rod and line. Hugh had watched him, intrigued, as he baited his hook with a daisy and then been amazed as within half an hour this clearly competent angler caught fifty frogs. He pronounced himself satisfied, thanked Hugh and departed with his catch.

I left the family in a sea of croissant crumbs the next morning to keep my appointment at the hairdresser. This is a great place to hear local gossip – if the customers, their heads in rows of rollers or wrapped in cling film, don't speak too quickly or lapse into patois. After declining to have my hair completely restyled, pressed to choose from a selection of photographs of models, alas, less than half my age, I managed to convince Madame that I simply wanted my roots retouched. Half an hour later, I was just beginning to understand an interesting conversation about the demise of the Monflanquin music festival when I was scooped up to the basin and my formerly attentive ears were filled with water.

My hair finished, at last – no one hurries here – the sky was a blazing blue outside the hairdresser's tinted window and I was anxious to leave. I had forgotten that Madame did not take a credit card and began to apologise, thinking that I would have to walk down the hill to the cash machine outside my bank, the Credit Agricole.

'*Mais non, Madame!*' she exclaimed, her delicately pencilled eyebrows disappearing under her lacquered fringe. '*Il y en a une en face.*'

I'd never noticed the machine across the road. I put in my Abbey National card and, as I casually folded

my Euros and turned to re-cross the road, I had a
sudden flash back to the dark days of '76 when we
bought Bel-Air. Almost with disbelief, I realised how
much had changed. It is so simple now to access
one's money from a 'hole in the wall' all over Europe,
and every week TV programmes actively encourage,
seduce even, potential buyers to borrow freely to buy
their dream home abroad. It seems barely credible
that thirty years ago we, among hundreds of British
pioneers, were made to feel guilty as we did our best
to beat the then-current punitive system.

In those austere days, far from being shown a
selection of desirable, completely restored properties
by a glamorous young enthusiast who promises to
complete most of the financial arrangements for you,
one had to spend weeks looking at highly undesirable
ruins. Handed a list by – often disinterested – agents
who seldom had even a photograph of the property
on offer it was quite an adventure, one certainly found
oneself in the most extraordinary places, but it was
very time-consuming. The greatest difference, however,
is that in those days, having found a house one had
first to apply to the bank of England for permission
even to buy abroad. Then it was necessary to pay a
severe dollar premium on one's own money on which,
of course, one had already paid income tax. It now
seems almost unbelievable but at that time, onto the
price of any potential property one had to automatically

add 40% for the hated premium, before considering the additional cost of agent's and solicitor's fees. It was just as well that the properties themselves were incredibly cheap but, nevertheless, everyone tried to circumnavigate the regulations in one way or another. Stories abounded. A useful asset, it was said, was an American friend with an English bank account who would do the deal for you and then be repaid. Another friend of a friend, more daring than we, took out the whole amount, filling her knickers with bundles of pesetas to buy an apartment in Torremolinas. Torremolinas has, of course, changed as much as the currency regulations since those days.

On a hot day in August '76, with a spruced-up Raymond and Claudette as the happy vendors, Mike and I sat in *Maître Fournon's* office, eager to become the new owners of Bel-Air, this long neglected house that we had just discovered. The office was cluttered with a great deal of dark wood panelling and smelt of polish. I remember the many photographs of rugby teams on the walls, serious fellows with rows of brawny arms folded above sturdy thighs. There was also something about the bulk of *Maître Fournon* and the width of his shoulders that suggested that he might in his youth have been more than just a spectator. Our French was not so good then and we made a great effort to understand not only the required documents but also all the conversation, which was rapid and with a strong local accent. As I remember it, somewhere between the team pictures and shelves of files there was also a notice to the effect that a *sous seing privé* on a purchase of a property was *Strictement Interdit*. This did not prevent us all from signing there and then just such a document.

Raymond, like every other Frenchman at that time with property to sell, was worried by a rumour that France was about to bring in a capital gains tax in the new year. Obviously they all wished to avoid this if they could and a great deal of cash was changing hands. At the very least, all vendors favoured the solution of declaring a slightly lower price than the buyer would actually pay. For the remainder, a private arrangement, '*sous la table*', a time-honoured tradition in France, would minimise the possible tax. For us, of course it would be an even greater saving. A private arrangement seemed eminently sensible and simple and *Maître Fournier* didn't bat an eyelid. Who am I, he seemed to imply, to collect taxes? As long as he got his fee he was content. Before we left for England that summer we arranged to bring down the rest of the money before Christmas, when the contracts for the exchange of the property would be ready for signing.

To amass even a small amount of French francs in London was not easy. The allowance of foreign currency in 1976 for an annual holiday was the equivalent of £100 each and had to be marked in one's passport. It seems like another world now, even the realisation that, then, not everyone went abroad automatically each year. Those of Mike's colleagues at Goldsmiths' college who preferred Dorset, or rural Wales perhaps, brought him small brown envelopes containing francs and were given sterling in exchange. As more and more ordinary people sought the adventure and challenge of buying abroad, friends and relations everywhere were being similarly pressed into service. Gradually our little pile of francs accumulated; now to get them down to Lot-et-Garonne. There were endless discussions about how, and where to hide them. The ideas got wilder. We met a couple just returned from a similar trip to the Loire valley, who had, they told us, lined their shoes with francs. Eventually Mike just pushed the bundle into his duffle coat pocket – ah, the duffle coat – and decided he would plead ignorance. It was all quite ridiculous.

We drove our camper down to Newhaven on a very wet and windy Thursday evening in late November. The large notice that greeted us on arrival in the customs house did nothing to calm our churning stomachs. In bold black letters it stated that anyone caught with over the limit of even English currency would not only have the sum confiscated but also their vehicle would be impounded. I seem to remember this limit being £25! Mike is no actor. He looked pale. Would he be guiltily silent, or, much more likely for a lecturer, would he talk too much?

'Just leave it to me,' I pleaded. But this was one role I did not relish.

At the very moment that we drove through customs there was a tremendous bang. We were so jumpy that we thought it must be to do with us. A currency-seeking device perhaps? The IRA? Whatever it was, it was unnerving. A sombre figure in a long, black, flapping raincoat came purposefully toward us. This was it. His pale face loomed closer. Lank black hair plastered his forehead.

'Hurry up,' he yelled, over the roar of the wind. 'They're just about to launch the lifeboat. Drive the van over there and you'll be able to see it.'

We sent up a prayer of thanksgiving as we watched the lifeboat set out into the dark, heaving sea. Then we drove our camper onto the ferry, parked it behind a couple of lorries and climbed up the swaying staircase into the saloon to celebrate. We were a little premature. The weather grew steadily worse and there was an announcement that the ferry was unable to leave. A communication had been sent to Arundel for a tug to pull us out of harbour but if this proved impossible, said the crackling voice over the tannoy, we might have to disembark and repeat the whole process the following day. We sat in a tense silence until it was announced that the tug had made it. We would soon be on our way. At last we unpacked our sandwiches, drank a toast and dozed fitfully on the lurching ship.

The bad weather followed us all down through France. We slept briefly in a lay-by but before dawn decided to resume our long journey. We finally gave up by early evening and stayed that night in a small hotel in Villereal, an ancient *bastide* town about ten miles from Bel-Air. We were exhausted. The next morning, after calling on *Maître Fournon* and signing the papers, we drove to Raymond's farm. On the way we stopped and recounted our little wad of money, just to make sure. The next time it was counted was on Raymond's kitchen table with the whole family, Grandma and Grandpa and the two children all gathered round.

'Where did you hide it?' asked Claudette.

'In my pocket,' said Mike nonchalantly. Grandpa whistled between his teeth. Then shook his head and laughed.

We heard later about a couple who hid a much larger amount in a talcum powder tin. All went as planned until their farmer took the notes to the bank. Being market day the bank was crowded and, as the teller fanned the notes with his thumb, the customers gazed in astonishment as he disappeared in a fine cloud of Johnson's baby powder!

I folded my so easily obtained Euros, walked back across the road and paid Madame. When I got back to Bel-Air the children were in the pool. I changed quickly to join them.

'Wow, Grandma, you look smart,' said Elliot. Then he shrieked with laughter as I jumped in and the carefully arranged hairdo was no more.

Matthew's brief stay was almost over. Bel-Air being *complet* and Judith due to arrive the night before his departure, when his brother Adam would gallantly drive him to catch the 6 a.m. TGV from Agen, we begged a bed for that night for Judith from our generous friend, Ruth Thomas.

Ruth and Edward Thomas also bought their house, about a mile away, in '76 and have proved kind and extremely hospitable summer neighbours. Long before we could afford a pool, we spent many happy hours in theirs and were always welcome to bring friends. Even Raymond was persuaded to try his first tentative strokes there and, afterwards, Edward always delighted in opening the Gosset, his favourite champagne.

On Matthew's last evening we planned a small celebration as his birthday was in a few days' time. We made a great variety of salads and barbecued small trout stuffed with garlic, salt and rosemary. I made a large chocolate cake, which is a family favourite, Claudette brought up a bowl of the last strawberries of the season, Ruth arrived with champagne.

Raymond gave Matthew a bottle of extremely *vieux* Cahors; from his diminishing store of dusty, unlabelled bottles laid down by Grandpa in the early fifties.

Inevitably, with wine so old, we have had the occasional disaster, but nine times out of ten when he opens one of these special bottles, the wine is sumptuous, almost black and with a flavour like no other wine. I am told that *vieux* Cahors is an acquired taste. I am just grateful that I have been privileged to acquire it.

Raymond was on good form. The first harvesting of the orchards had been completed. Although a great many plums had been knocked down by the heavy rain they were large and unharmed by falling – that it was thanks to Jean-Michel, I forbore to mention!

It wouldn't be such a bad harvest after all, he agreed, and of course, the rain would be good for the maize and the vines, and the grazing cattle; the great advantage of '*la polyculture*'. As Claudette dished out the strawberries and the children debated whether to have coconut ice cream before or after the cake –Thomas favoured both – Raymond was reminded of the story of the old *Curé* and the village fountain.

'*Vous n'avez jamais entendu ça?*' he said in surprise. Then his eyes shone at the chance of telling us a joke. '*Il était une fois un certain village,*' he began dramatically. Apparently their *Curé* had, tactfully, for the purpose of their confessions, invented a euphemism for a marital lapse on the part of the women in the village.

'Not that they were a particularly promiscuous lot,' Raymond explained with a shrug. Claudette pursed her lips and raised her eyebrows. '*Mais non!*'

insisted Raymond. *'C'était une question de délicatesse.'*
Claudette giggled. *'Alors,* when they came to confession,'
continued Raymond. 'It was not necessary to go into
details. The gentle *Curé* suggested that, as long as the
sinner was truly repentant, they should simply say *'J'ai
glissé à la Fontaine,'* I slipped at the fountain. This
would suffice, he would understand, forgive and name
a suitable penance. This custom continued for so many
years, it passed into the language until eventually the
old *Curé* died. The new, young *Curé* was puzzled.
He went to the Mayor. *'Monsieur le Maire,'* he said.
'Something must be done about the fountain.' The
Mayor expressed surprise. The *Curé* insisted. 'Perhaps
it is the steps,' he suggested. 'When the women go to
get water they are always slipping over.'

'Nonsense!' declared the Mayor.

'Nonsense, is it?' cried the *Curé*. 'Why, your own
wife slipped over twice last week!'

We translated an edited version for Thomas. Elliot
was, as usual, in a world of his own. We drank toasts;
one for Matthew and his coming birthday, another
for Mike, looking so much better and grateful for his
continuing recovery. Then, sadly, we toasted our old
friends, Barry and Edward, no longer with us but so
much a part of our memories of gatherings of friends
at Bel-Air.

CHAPTER ELEVEN

The days flew by as they always do when the family are at Bel-Air and all too soon it was their last market day. We arranged to meet Jonathan, Miranda and Abie, who were also leaving for England in a few days' time, at our usual rendezvous, Le Winger, the bar in Libos market. As the weather was not promising, instead of a picnic at Bel-Air, we decided to take them all out to lunch to a restaurant we thought they would enjoy.

It was in the very early years at Bel-Air when we first discovered the Hôtel Climat, as it was then called, nestling at the bottom of the square behind the church in Fumel. Its centrally heated, spotlessly clean and simple, modern interior was a welcome change on cold evenings in spring when our house was still in a very primitive condition and we had been labouring in the garden all day. When the temperature had plummeted with the setting sun, the wind had begun to whistle under the door and the fire had almost gone out, we would spruce ourselves up, put hot water bottles in the bed and set off to dine very cheaply in what, by comparison with our unrestored interior, felt like extreme luxury.

Now renamed Hôtel Kyriad, it is, as before, extremely well managed by a sweet-faced Madame Anne-Marie Julien, originally from Holland, and her French husband. Some of the staff have changed over the years but they take their cue from Madame and are always friendly. I still remember an elderly waiter in a rusty black jacket who, one lunchtime, when I was not particularly hungry, introduced me to the cheapest way to eat there. The restaurant has self-service buffets of hors d'oeuvre and of desserts, each costing only, at that time, 30 francs.

'For only 60 francs, Madame,' he said gently, 'you can choose and eat as much or as little as you like.' He shrugged and smiled. 'Why bother with *le menu* today?'

It was quite a revelation when, for the first time, we went to the restaurant during the day. We ate outside on the terrace at the rear of the building. The view from there stretches down across the panorama of the Lot valley and up to the splendid trees in the gardens of the Hôtel de Ville, once the Château of the Seigneur de Fumel. The Château, home of a noble family since the eleventh century, was rebuilt in the sixteenth century in the same flamboyant style as the Palais du Louvres. Unfortunately for the family they fell foul of the local populace in the long and bitter wars of religion, and the Seigneur was brutally murdered. The beautiful terraced garden, designed in the eighteenth century, can still be visited.

The small town of Fumel is now known chiefly as the site of the only heavy industry in the area. The iron foundry, which draws its power from a barrage built over the river at the base of the town, still provides a great deal of employment. During the war it was from one of the offices at the factory, where many of the workers were Communists, that, in March 1943, members of the local Resistance were recruited. The accounts of their activities, kept in the archives at Bordeaux, make interesting reading.

The group were extremely well organised. They had small English radios which had been parachuted in, as well as arms which were hidden in nearby farms all over the region. Morning and evening liaisons were established but very soon one of their leaders, Conti, was arrested by the Gestapo and they were forced to lie low for a while. When they resumed their activities, as a further precaution, the parachute drops were given code names. They were somewhat literary, being *'Gauthier'* and *'Honoré'*.

The messages to be passed identifying the location were *'les feuilles sont chassées par la tempête'* (the leaves are chased by the storm), indicating that the drop was at *'Gauthier'*. *'Si seulement vous vouliez m'aider'* (if only you would help me) told the listeners that it was to be at *'Honoré'*. They set ambushes and immobilised many trains by simply blowing up the wheels on the front and back wagons.

One of their more daring and successful exploits was the capturing of weapons and ammunition from the Gendarmerie at Villeneuve. Tipped off by a sympathetic gendarme at Fumel they set off in convoy, at one point hiding in the high ground at Penne while a German convoy passed by on the road beneath them. They arrived at Villeneuve at 11.45 a.m., turning their lorries in order to be able to leave at speed. As they relieved the gendarmes of all their weapons they describe the mixed reactions of the police, some hiding their approval, others clearly unsympathetic to the Allied cause. It was market day in Villeneuve and they loaded up their booty; 23 light machine rifles, six revolvers, a large quantity of ammunition and three brand new Simca sidecars, to the cheers of the watching crowds. They also warned them of an approaching German column with a group of the hated Milices – French police loyal to the Nazis – so the Resistance beat a hasty retreat back to Fumel, no doubt well pleased with themselves. But it was a dangerous game. There are many small memorials beside the roads to mark the spot where a brave partisan met his fate. M. René, our old builder, who helped us so much when we first started work on the house, still reminisces about his days helping the Resistance. Today, the factory workers amble out at the end of the day, and climb on their bicycles to ride home peacefully.

The Hôtel Kyriad added an infinity pool to the small terraced garden, the first I had ever seen. I imagined floating right over the edge. I've never actually seen anyone swimming in it. Perhaps guests staying in the hotel take an early morning dip. We introduced Raymond and Claudette to the restaurant. They were impressed and came occasionally during the winter – a rare treat for them. Their two menus, which between the unlimited choice of starters and puddings always include a simple but well cooked *entrée,* with a demi pitcher of house wine, cost them only 27 Euros together. As they said *'Pour le prix, c'est remarquable!'*

Changing from one hotel chain to another didn't seem to change anything else. I imagine that Kyriad, the new owners, who have apparently more than 160 hotels in Europe, recognised a successful manager. The restaurant is usually full. There are not many English – it is not ethnic enough for the tourist; no rough stone walls decorated with ancient farm implements;

no *confit de canard,* or *lapin aux pruneaux* on the menu. We, of course, don't mind this. Those we can eat *chez* Claudette.

As we strolled through the market that morning, the clouds thickened. Not much chance of the sun breaking through for a few hours, we thought, and were glad we had decided to eat indoors. Perhaps if it cleared up later the kids would all get a late swim. Le Winger was crowded but Abie soon spotted us. After the boys had raced about and downed their Cokes, they took their turn at the table football. There's always a queue on market days. Fair shares of time are carefully checked by small, sunburnt, beady-eyed children. They stand all down the sides of the table, elbows on the edge, chins propped on their hands, watching the players. At last we prized them away and, our shopping completed, thought about lunch.

Abie decided to ride with our two boys. I went off with Jonathan and Miranda to another of the many car parks, which surround the town, but with which I was unfamiliar, to show them the way to the restaurant. Cars were already leaving as we arrived. The 'nose bag panic' as a friend of mine calls it. That determined, almost manic rush to eat, no matter what else is happening, that seizes the French, once the midday bell, or siren, has sounded. Market traders, unless they are North African, will pack up and leave, even if still faced with a queue of customers. For twenty minutes or so the roads are crammed with drivers, seemingly desperate to eat. While our car park emptied as if by magic, we too began to feel hungry. The only problem was that Jonathan's car refused to start.

'Don't worry,' said Miranda airily. 'It sometimes does this. Just ignore it for a few seconds and it will be OK.'

The few seconds turned into more than a few minutes but still the car, a fairly new Renault people-carrier, did not respond. As the remaining cars began to leave, the last stragglers starting their engines without difficulty and racing across to the exit, we began to worry. There we stood, bonnet up, looking at the engine without the vaguest idea what to do. Fortunately, the last car on its way out of the vast, empty car park stopped. The driver got out and joined us.

He was English, charming, accompanied by his wife and with two little girls in the back of his car. He clearly knew a bit about engines but nothing would start ours into life. How could they help? They obviously felt bad about just abandoning us. I didn't have the number of the hotel, neither was I sure about the number for directory enquiries. We knew that the others, waiting patiently to order, would begin to worry. By luck, our good samaritans turned out to be on their way to visit the Château of Bonaguil. Did we know how to get there? We did, and this was fortunate, as they needed to go into Fumel and past the Hotel Kyriad. They offered me a lift.

For some reason, I'm not quite sure now why, Jonathan insisted on unloading from his car into theirs the things he had borrowed from us that summer. He was very concerned to return them before they packed up and left. There was also a large cake in a box, a present from Miranda and a last minute purchase of a long stick of celery.

Madame was at her desk in the small elegant foyer, when I struggled in, balancing the celery on the cake box, my arm through a large coil of dirty yellow garden hose, the other wielding a heavy chainsaw. As I tried to explain she pealed with laughter. 'Don't worry,' she said. 'Just put them anywhere. You must be very hungry.'

The rest of the family looked relieved to see me. I was indeed hungry but Adam immediately volunteered to return to the car park to fetch Jonathan and Miranda, who he reckoned would be equally so. The only problem was that, as he had no idea where the car park was, I had to postpone my order and return with him. Jonathan, meanwhile, had managed to phone the emergency services only to be told that everyone was at lunch. Of course! With relief we all set off again to the restaurant, the ever-patient staff by now enjoying the drama. Hardly had Jonathan begun his starter when his phone rang. An angry voice said, 'I've left my meal, Monsieur, I am at your car. Where are you?'

Adam's taxi service was once more in operation. While I managed to begin my meal and the boys chose yet another pudding, Adam and a gloomy Jonathan watched the mechanic doing his best. Nothing, however, would persuade the Renault to start and it was finally towed away to a garage and we all trooped back to finish our meal in an almost deserted dining room.

With only one car between nine of us there was nothing for it but to return to Bel-Air in relays. My daughter-in-law, Caz, and I enjoyed walking back about two kilometres to the bar where we were later picked up. Back at Bel-Air, at last, we all sat down to a strong cup of tea. As they had no means of getting home, Jonathan and Co. moved into the green room, much to the boys' delight. The sun came out and we all swam. Mike managed twenty lengths and got a cheer.

The next day was spent to-ing and fro-ing to the garage. By late afternoon and many, 'Ah, Monsieur, dans une heure, c'est possible, mais...' type of responses it became increasingly clear that the problem with the car was complicated. Raymond came past on the tractor with a load of plums and tut-tutted sympathetically. 'Et *c'est une marque Française,*' he said ruefully, adding that we were all invited down to the farm later for dessert.

After supper the children went for yet another swim. As always they were reluctant to get out of the pool and Claudette phoned at just after eight-thirty to ask where we were. I was surprised, as dessert on the farm is usually a movable feast, anytime up to ten p.m. We gathered the children, hurried them into their clothes and all piled into our, fortunately large, estate car, the boys giggling in the boot as we went very slowly down the bumpy track.

We soon saw why she had phoned. Raymond stood in his striped jersey waiting to take Miranda and Jonathan and the children out for a trip in the old Citroën before it got too dark. Off they went, roaring across the courtyard, while we sat peacefully enjoying one of last year's prunes in *Eau de Vie,* tipped into our still-warm coffee cup. The next day a hire car was organised, our guests left to pack up their house and we drove our family to Agen to catch the TGV to Paris. The boys loaded up their back packs, their golf clubs and bags. Many kisses and waves reached us from the window as we watched the great, smooth, powerful train pull out. They were gone. As we drove back from Agen we caught the strong scent of marigolds as the first dusty fields of brown, ripe sunflowers were being harvested.

Bel-Air seemed awfully quiet. Our temporary but inevitable sadness was comforted by the thought of several very peaceful days before our next guests would arrive.

CHAPTER TWELVE

The group of old friends who were coming to stay would be our last visitors of the summer and, even as we prepared for their arrival, we were beginning to plan our journey home to London. Mike was feeling so much stronger that we decided not to put the car on the train. We so enjoy almost always choosing a different route to and from Bel-Air. While others boast about doing the entire journey in just so many hours, we, who of course have the great advantage of ten, or even twelve weeks ahead of us, take several days coming; staying in and exploring interesting areas.

Some places merit a second visit. One such is Fontevraud. Here the effigies of Eleanor of Aquitaine, her husband Henry II and her son, Richard the Lionheart, lie in state on the tomb of the Plantagenets.

I have always been fascinated by Eleanor; intelligent

and highly educated child of Poitou, the land of romance and troubadours. The girl who, aged barely fifteen, wed the seventeen-year-old heir to the throne of France, the pale, ascetic young Louis. At first Eleanor captivated her young husband, while shocking most of the court in Paris, including her mother-in-law, with her exotic 'southern' ways. She followed him dutifully on crusades with a retinue of maids, chests full of dresses and jewels and a troupe of musicians to entertain her. But once she had set eyes on the handsome, virile and highly intelligent Henri, Duke of Anjou and Normandy, almost ten years her junior, she was determined to marry him. She set about obtaining an annulment of her marriage to Louis and two months later in the spring of 1152 she and Henri were quietly married. Two years later the young Duke became Henry II, one of England's most successful kings and she his radiant queen. She bore him six children and the first years of their marriage were happy. When Henry eventually tired of her, she was a virtual prisoner in England until, on Henry's death, she returned at last to her beloved France. She took the veil and became Abbess of Fontevraud but, until the last days of her turbulent life, she continued to involve herself in the political ambitions of her children and grandchildren.

Another town that we have revisited is Chauvigny. The Hotel Lion d'Or is very comfortable and the cuisine excellent but what we enjoy most is to walk in the late afternoon sunshine up and up into the old city. The interior of the Église Saint-Pierre is a painted miracle with capitals of wonderfully carved animals; curly-maned lions, back-to-back, and a winged bull with fearsome claws. If you wish, you can watch real eagles fly from the ramparts.

The only other town we have visited twice is La Flèche. It was not chasing history this time but the recommendation of a good hotel and an excellent restaurant that drew us there initially. Le Relais Cicero was, we were assured, something special. It seemed worth driving just that little bit further to spend the first night in a really quiet hotel and eat at the intriguingly named *La Fesse d'Ange*. The 'Angel's Bum' was, we were also told, two minutes walk from the hotel and the food extremely good. We booked, just to be sure.

We found La Flèche itself without difficulty and drove into the square. The Relais Cicero was at number eighteen, Boulevard Alger, a turning to the right. But there was no right turn. Facing us, the square was filled with a monumental building. As we turned, inevitably, left, I read over the great doorway the, to me, mysterious word *Prytanée*. As we then turned right and continued for about half a mile alongside this walled building we realised how vast a space in the centre of the town it occupied. It was clearly something to be investigated later. Having completed the square we finally found le Relais Cicero almost hidden in a garden.

The hotel was originally a seventeenth century convent, later converted to a bourgeois house and furnished accordingly. There is an elegant annexe of a slightly later period but we were able to stay in the original part. Our room was huge with incredibly ornate wallpaper, brocaded armchairs, a wonderfully large bed and crossed swords over the mantelpiece. The winding staircases creaked and there were very old books laid out to read in all the reception rooms. The restaurant, *La Fesse d'Ange,* was reached from the garden by passing through a courtyard and under an archway. I can't remember what we ate. I have only a memory of something delicate, exquisite sauces and tall, rather aristocratic and willowy waitresses. The whole experience was – what shall I say? I suppose 'angelic' might be the appropriate word.

In our quiet room overlooking the garden we slept later than usual. We had intended to investigate the *Prytanée* which we had learnt was a military academy, but we lingered over breakfast in the panelled dining room and couldn't resist some of the beautiful and fascinating books just lying around. After eventually checking out we found that we would have to wait for a guided tour of *La Prytanée* which would itself last over an hour. As we had arranged to spend the next night with friends a good day's drive further on, we reluctantly decided that a full appreciation of La Flêche, clearly a very interesting town on *le Loire* would have to wait for another year. A repeat performance at both the hotel and the restaurant would be no hardship.

On our second visit we resisted the sleepy charm of the bedroom with the crossed swords and presented ourselves early next morning at the great doorway of the *Prytanée*. A row of extremely smart cadets sprang to attention and one was designated to be our guide. As we passed through the series of wonderful buildings and courtyarded gardens we learnt that they were originally founded as a Jesuit college by Henri IV. There were separate buildings designated for different uses. There was the *'salle des actes'*, where the pupils of the Jesuits were taught the art of public oratory, and the wonderful Chapel where their religious duties were performed. The church is extremely beautiful with a great deal of marble and jasper. Henri IV bequeathed his heart and that of his wife Marie de Medici into the keeping of the Jesuits. Elaborate niches were designed in which the hearts were placed, but they were destroyed during the revolution and the hearts burnt. Today there remain only the ashes in a heart-shaped reliquary. The Jesuits were expelled from France in 1782 and the college began to take on its present function as a military academy. It is named after the Prytaneum of the ancient Greeks in Athens where the sacred flame was kept alight and where the most distinguished men were admitted. Today's young men are preparing for entry into the *grandes écoles militaires* in an institution where the great philosopher Descartes was educated, but our fresh-faced and gallant young guide was, endearingly, more keen to explain the tradition of the cadets pushing each other into the pond on graduation.

Over the years Raymond kept telling us about a visit he and Claudette had made to a place called Puy du Fou. They had gone on an organised coach trip and he urged us to visit it on one of our journeys south. As far as we could gather it was a *'son et lumière'* spectacle.

'Oh, c'est magnifique!' he had said. *'C'est vraiment quelque chose à voir. C'est l'histoire de la Vendée. Quatorze mille spectateurs!'*

Mike wasn't sure that he wanted to go anywhere with 14,000 other people but I was intrigued. As we prepared our next summer trip I saw that Puy du Fou lay south-east of Nantes. We could make a slight detour on our downward journey I thought, and see what it was that had so excited Raymond. I planned a route that would, I hoped, get us somewhere near there on our second night.

The first night we stayed at Château-Gontier. We didn't book but the Hostellerie de Mirwault looked interesting in the Guide Michelin. Just out of town and by the river Mayenne, it sounded promising. We drove over the bridge into the town and turned right following a sign.

'Are you sure we haven't missed it?' asked Mike as we continued some distance down a winding road. But no, we turned into a drive and there it was, right on the edge of the river. The hotel was an addition onto a much older building and the rooms were in a modern, well-furnished, single storey annexe. Apart from one other couple we were the only guests. It was incredibly quiet. The hotel seemed to be run by only two staff: a very pretty dark-skinned blonde and a young boy. They moved quietly and efficiently about but did not speak unless spoken to. The food was good but not extraordinary, the bed very large and comfortable.

The next day was Wednesday and market day in Château-Gontier, and we lingered until midday before making our way south-westward towards Puy du Fou only to learn that we were out of luck. The spectacle only took place at the weekends. I was annoyed with myself for not realising that, as the huge cast was composed of local people, this was likely to be so. We consoled ourselves by eating like lords in La Rochelle. At least we were seeing a different region of this amazing country. We decided to go on down the west coast through *le Marais* with its lakes and streams. Sunflowers seemed to have caught on here too. Once they were only grown in the real south. Now, with new varieties developed, they march in splendour ever northwards.

The town of Blaye, on the Gironde, looked an interesting idea. As we drove in it looked even more intriguing but, alas, Blaye was *complet*. Every room had been taken for *'Le Jumping National'*. We continued our journey south and finally arrived at the tiny Hotel Saint Christophe in Bourg sur Gironde. The hotel was friendly, quiet and cheap with a good restaurant just across the road. The local wine cooperative proved also to be a place in which to linger, sample and buy the excellent *Côte de Bourg*. And so, without having seen Raymond's *'spectacle'* but with a few interesting bottles for him to show that we had at least tried, we made our way eastward to Bel-Air. We stopped for lunch at Allemans-du-Dropt, another riverside town with one of the most attractive picnic spots I know.

I resolved to arrange things better the following summer and in July, before we left London, I telephoned to book for the spectacle at Puy du Fou in three weeks' time.

'Mais, Madame, c'est tout complet,' was the response.

'All fourteen thousand seats?!'

'Oui, Madame.'

'Any hope for the following night?' I enquired

'Désolé, Madame, mais c'est complet pour toute la saison,' was the reply.

Clearly Puy du Fou was something of a phenomenon

or the marketing was superb, or both.

We decided nevertheless, to travel via Château-Gontier again and stay in what I had named the 'ghost hotel'. It was such a peaceful place to spend the first night after all the traumas of packing up in London, catching the ferry, and getting through Caen; although the sheer wonder of crossing the Seine by the *Pont de Normandie* always lifts my spirits. Our bedroom in the Hostellerie de Mirwault was just as charming, with elegant fabrics, bottled water, an orange on a plate. We sipped an aperitif in the garden beneath a huge tree – a *cedrus atlantica*, planted, so the label said, between 1650 and 1700. We strolled along by the river where small cottages were hung with petunias, then turned back to the hotel, watching the insects hovering above the dark water, smooth as glass before it reached the weir.

In the hotel itself there were vases of scented lilies. Beautiful bone china bowls and tureens decorated the restaurant. This time it appeared that we were the only clients and we moved into the small dining area at the far end, which is the oldest part of the building. Originally a pavilion café, it is six-sided and its three long windows overlook the weir. The dying sunlight lit up the far bank as we began our meal in this dream-like place. We ate a salad with *lardons* and *gésiers,* which was followed by a very good steak with *morilles*. The cheese board came with walnuts and the dessert was *tarte aux poires et myrtilles*. The whole tranquil experience cost us 280 francs and we never saw the patron or anyone else. The young boy to whom we paid our modest bill in the morning told us that the patron was English but not often there. It remains a mystery. Unable to see the spectacle at Puy du Fou, we continued south to visit another kind of spectacle of which I never tire. The wonderful 14th-century tapestries of the Apocalypse in the Chateau d'Angers are even better lit and displayed than before. We sat mesmerised for about an hour, then joined a guided tour. There is always some exquisite detail to be discovered.

The following year, absolutely determined to get to the spectacle at Puy du Fou, I booked our seats just after Easter. It seemed prudent to also book a hotel, but for one night only in three months' time. The proprietor of the hotel, La Terrasse in Mauléon was quite unperturbed.

'*Oui. Oui, vous irez au spectacle sans doute,*' he said. 'We'll give you a key to come in late.'

The hotel was small, comfortable and totally unlike our 'ghost hotel', being completely full and everything overseen by an affable patron. There was a real air of excitement among the diners that evening, many of them with teenage children. We set off into the dark without much idea of what to expect. The brochure was fairly lurid. During daylight hours there was also, we learnt, *a parc historique et écologique* covering 30 hectares, complete with a recreated 18th-century village and displays of falconry and horsemanship. We thought that *le spectacle* might suffice.

As we drove about twelve kilometres through the dark, it seemed bizarre to think that all this activity was hidden somewhere deep in this silent and thickly wooded countryside. As cars began to converge and we turned, following clear signs, up a well-made, tree-lined road we began to appreciate just how well organised was the whole affair. Red jacketed and smiling marshals appeared, to wave us on. Others directed us to swift and efficient parking in a vast, well-lit clearing in the forest. Hundreds of cars and coaches were already neatly lined up. People scrambled out of their cars clutching jackets and rugs. Children stowed drinks, packets of sweets and crisps in their pockets. More smiling stewards pointed the way and we followed a steady stream of people along a small, softly lit, woodland path. There were no queues, no bottlenecks.

I gasped at the height of the great stadium with its tiers of seats. There was a wide escalator to take us gently to the top where we walked along and then down to our numbered section. The show was supposed to start at ten p.m., but it was a question of waiting until it was completely dark. We could still just discern the outline of a Château and the gleam of a lake. Gangs of local young people appeared to entertain us, scruffy and yet stylish in a way that only French teenagers seem to manage. They clowned and did handstands and cartwheels along the front of the stands. They encouraged the crowd in rhythmic clapping and Mexican waves. It was all good-humoured and as the last light faded away, so did they.

I don't know quite what I expected. A spectacle! 800 actors from fifteen neighbouring communities, 50 horsemen, lasers and fountains – it was all in the brochure. What was stunning was the sudden plunge into complete darkness, the silence, and then the small trembling light from a single lantern, carried by a figure moving across the landscape. This was Jacques Maupillier, the archetypal peasant from the region, la Vendée, through whose eyes the whole story was told, using the recorded voices of Philippe Noiret and other actors. As the trudging figure moved on, a small dwelling was revealed, a family sitting round the table. The traveller knocked and entered and told them the news of the coming troubles, which would eventually lead up to the great Revolution. We saw the news brought to a whole village, complete with animals and children. Each scene was set in the dark and then brilliantly lit. We sat enthralled as later the great Château was illuminated with music and revelry. People arrived by boat on the lake. Elegantly costumed dancers whirled and swayed in the windows.

I knew that this part of France was fiercely Catholic and many of the peasants still maintained an almost feudal loyalty to their local noble families. As the Revolution progressed they saw that it was the bourgeoisie in the towns who were benefiting; not the peasants. 300,000 rose against the new Republic, hoping that England would help them. But they were defeated and cruelly massacred by Republican soldiers. We watched as troops of horsemen arrived at full gallop towards the Château. Shots were fired. Battles were lost and won. Prisoners were led away. The great Château burned, the flames leaping into the sky. I can't pretend I followed the significance of every scene. Considering how long it had taken me to organise this visit, I cursed myself for not having better done my homework on the history of La Vendée.

But Raymond was right. It was something to be seen. The cast were impeccable. Whoever produced and directed this level of discipline with hundreds of amateur performers had to be a genius. There were celebrations, funerals, battles and scenes of lyrical beauty. A great crowd of peasants made hay in the evening sunlight, loading the heavy carts to be pulled away by quiet horses. The show lasted almost two hours and ended with a splendid finale of fountains and fireworks. I shall always remember the final great parade of peasants complete with children, leading all their animals across the wide arena to cheers and prolonged applause. Horses, cows, sheep, pigs, goats and even geese; all bathed in a golden light, all of whom seemed to know exactly what to do. And when it was all over, we left, row by row. Once again there were no queues. The same helpful marshals, surely tired by now, were on hand to direct us, to speed us out into the dark and starry night. I'm afraid that the *navigateur,* drunk with the spectacle, took us, temporarily, on the wrong road. But that's another story – best not told.

When, some years later, I went to see the Dome, I thought what an opportunity had been lost. I imagined the history of London, in *son et lumière,* using the river, and hundreds of local people in just such a way, and felt that it could have been a real *spectacle* with which to celebrate the millennium.

CHAPTER THIRTEEN

'*La pluie ce soir!*' yelled M. Gouyou over the noise of his tractor as he passed the house that afternoon. He was right. By eight o'clock the lake between the green room door and the shower room was filling relentlessly. Thankful that our friends were not due for another few days, we prayed that it would soon stop and that before we left at the end of this summer M. Carpentier would arrive to finally solve the problem. Round the house and down the pathway the rain ran off the baked, stony ground, but the following morning we noticed that it had made deep furrows in Jean-Michel's new track across the field.

The pathway which runs past our house is a *chemin communal* and we are entitled, every two years, to a load of stones paid for by the commune, to help maintain it. When we first bought Bel-Air, the handsome *géomètre* who arrived with his giant tape measure, to mark out our exact piece of land surrounding the house, found an anomaly. After consulting the *cadastre,* his detailed survey map, he discovered that, years before and without permission, Raymond had simply altered the position of the track so that it ran behind, rather than in front of Bel-Air. I imagine that it made easier access with ever-larger machines; but no one, neither Raymond, nor Grandpa, had thought to inform the authorities. Raymond probably simply forgot. Grandpa had little use for authority, other than his own. Once discovered however, French bureaucracy demanded an immediate redrawing of the map. This, in its turn, necessitated an '*acte*' to be passed by the Mayor. It was one of the reasons that our deeds took longer than expected to be finalised, while Raymond, still anxious about the possibility of a capital gains tax, fretted.

Jean-Michel took no chances this time – his wife is, after all, the Deputy Mayor! But half of the track he wished to change lay in the next commune and another Mayor had to be consulted. Our former charmer of a Mayor of this commune having recently retired after long years of service, we now have an equally charming *Madame la Maire*. I imagine the two women just put their heads together and sorted things out amicably.

The reason for wanting to change things this time

was that the *chemin*, which ran from our house right down to the road, passed through the middle of Jean-Michel and Véronique's farm, between the great barn and the house. Although the traffic is minimal – the odd van, a slow-moving tractor; at weekends the occasional, intrepid pair of helmeted teenagers on incredibly noisy, small *mobylettes* would suddenly loom into view. One Sunday a couple of quad bikes thundered by, the drivers waving gaily. That was enough for Jean-Michel. With Océane playing outside, not to mention a dog, a cat and the odd wandering fowl, he set about devising another route, which would bypass their farm.

He had told us about it the previous year and we were intrigued when we first arrived this summer to see PROPRIETÉ PRIVÉE as we crossed the little bridge at the bottom of his drive. A smaller, more discreet sign pointed the different route now to be followed up to Bel-Air. The new *chemin* snaked across the bottom of the field where the cows graze and then mounted between Raymond's land and that of his neighbour, M. Guyou.

'*Oh, c'est pas pour vous,*' said Jean-Michel, the next morning. '*C'est pour les autres.*' But we use it just the same. They are entitled to their privacy. It's a little longer and this morning would be very muddy, but the view is lovely.

Jean-Michel and Véronique have worked hard on the house since they first moved in after their marriage.

As well as being a competent farmer, Jean-Michel is no mean builder, carpenter, painter or decorator. Véronique loves to buy pieces of old furniture at *brocante* fairs and do them up. She has also created a lovely garden. I envy her a magnificent apricot-coloured, repeat-flowering rose, which scrambles up the wooden support to the barn. But, of course, she does have an unlimited, on site, supply of manure. With her duties as Deputy Mayor and working eight hour shifts at Auchan, the hypermarket in Villeneuve sur Lot, I also envy her energy.

In August of 2001 we received an unexpected and intriguing invitation.

'*10 ANS DE MARIAGE, VOILÀ LE RÉSULTAT...*' was the caption on a photograph of the three of them in a field of poppies. Jean-Michel, shirt-sleeved, resolute, one arm bent to his waist, gazing into the future; Véronique, bare arms, squatting among the flowers, in a then-trendy, lime green jump suit, smiling up into the camera and Océane, ebullient as ever, arms flung wide, laughing as she throws petals into the air. Superimposed on the photograph were pictures of a large mother cow and two calves. *FAMILLE NOMBREUSE!!!* written below.

The invitation was to '*faire la fête a partir de 20 heures*' at the *Salle des Fêtes* at St Aubin, a nearby village.

The *salle* is new and spacious and can easily hold

several hundred guests. It has a fully equipped kitchen with several fridges and a large freezer. There is a long, elegant bar, a wide stage, unlimited tables and chairs and a vast, tiled floor for dancing. To *faire la fête* in this area, no matter how small the commune, is a serious business.

Once the invitations were sent out, we were all roped in to help prepare what was clearly going to be a copious buffet. The afternoon before the celebration the smell of roasting pork filled Claudette's kitchen. Raymond staggered about with crates of salad. As always, there was a certain air of competition. Tenth wedding anniversary celebrations were apparently the fashion. Someone had been to one in the same *salle* three weeks previously. Menus were discussed. Mike and I were on parade early the next morning. Claudette's kitchen tables, both inside and outside, were all in use. Véronique, her hair screwed up with an elastic band, was busy with an electric carver, slicing the long, rolled joints of pork and arranging them on silver trays. Claudette, with a giant wooden spoon, was stirring mayonnaise into vast quantities of potato salad. I must have made enough carrot salad to feed the whole of south-west France using a borrowed machine that jammed about every third carrot. It was a swine to dismantle and re-assemble but it saved one's fingernails.

Jean-Michel's stalwart mother arrived with a huge

tray of pizza and a plate of still-defrosting *pain poisson*. This, she explained, as she cut it carefully into slices, was made with a mixture of salmon, tuna, crab and eggs and then baked. It smelt delicious. We prepared tray after tray of tomato salad, cucumber salad, using clingfilm by the mile, and wondered what we did before it was invented. We broke briefly for a lunch of bread, wine, and the well-cooked ends of the joints. Delicious! A nibble of cheese, fruit, and we were off again. After two or three trips to the *salle*, the back of our estate car filled with long trays of food to unload into the fridge, we finally left another team laying the tables and went back to Bel-Air for a rest and a bath.

There were about 150 guests and so many snacks with the aperitifs that I wondered whether the buffet would get eaten. I needn't have worried. It was a really good evening with a great mixture of friends and family. The walls were decorated with photographs of Véronique in her wedding dress and Jean-Michel looking incredibly smart. I remembered the sudden storm late that afternoon ten years ago that had us all scurrying for cover, Véronique with her dress looped over her arm and Claudette running to save the decorations she had so patiently made. As we looked at pictures of Océane as a baby, we caught up with members of both families that we hadn't seen for several years. Claudette's cousins Roland and

Nicole, both gymnasts, were there. With their three beautiful children, they had come to teach Raymond and Claudette to swim when we first had our pool. Ken and Sandra, our nearest English neighbours, were there with friends. They all shouted for me to sing and I was glad I'd warmed up with a few scales in the bath. Old habits die hard. I sang and enjoyed myself. We stayed till past 4 a.m. and I realised how much we are a part of this community.

I watched Corinne, Raymond's beautiful daughter-in-law, dancing with her handsome brother Louis. Like their mother, they both love to dance and are very good at it. Later I watched Corinne persuade Philippe onto the floor. She smiled as she danced, taunted and coaxed him, flaunting her slim body with its perfect curves. Philippe is like Claudette. He finds it hard to let go, but this wife of his was irresistible and at last he responded and we saw a different Philippe, dancing with the same wild fervour. It made me very happy to watch them. Jean-Michel doesn't dance but he is content to sit and watch Véronique. Both Raymond's children seem to have very good marriages – for which we are all thankful.

The next morning we were invited back to the *salle* to eat *les restes* and, of course, to help clear up. We knew the form from previous occasions. One table, amid all the chaos abandoned from the festivities, had been cleared and about twenty of us sat down to eat. There seemed no lack of enthusiasm for the still-delicious remains. Jean-Michel had even brought a special jeroboam of good red wine. I was intrigued to see that it was Corinne, who having slept, so she told me, till past midday, came in late but soon took charge.

Once we had finished eating, our small army simply folded the gay paper tablecloths in halves, shovelling everything into black plastic sacks. Paper plates, picnic glasses, designer napkins, candles and cutlery entwined with streamers, vanished. Only the table decorations of fresh flowers were carefully put into a box to be distributed among us. While we, the women, made sure that the kitchen was as we had originally found it, the men and the boys took over in the hall; snapping down table legs and stacking them and building tall columns of chairs at great speed. We came back to see Jean-Michel's brother-in-law and two friends armed with brooms a metre across sweeping in tight formation the vast expanse of floor. Next they threw down buckets of hot water and, in bare feet and wielding equally large squeegees, they worked as a team until the whole place was spotless. It was very impressive.

The rain had stopped. The lake outside the green room door was subsiding slowly and the sun reappeared. As I sat under the porch watching the steam rising off the vineyard, I wondered what they would do for their twentieth anniversary and whether I would be here to see it.

Later the following evening we telephoned Raymond. We'd been keeping watch. *'Ils sont arrivés,'* we said.

'Les étourneaux?'

'Oui.'

'Merde!' was his response. *'Je vais chercher le canon.'*

There were already blue plastic ribbons at intervals tied among the rows in this the newest vineyard, which we see from our front door. Raymond had placed great faith in these strips blowing in the breeze. For some reason, he was of the opinion that *les étourneaux* – the starlings – did not like blue and would avoid it. With the vines already heavy with succulent grapes, which were growing larger and riper every day, I thought the birds might think them worth any affront to their appreciation of colour. Every year *les étourneaux* seem to arrive around the beginning of September. They sweep in great wheeling clouds across the fields and if they are exceptionally numerous can decimate a crop. Fortunately they don't seem to stay very long so it is more a question of persuading them to fly off somewhere else. For this the cannon was now to be brought into use. It would shatter the silence once every ten or fifteen minutes, causing the birds to fly up in alarm. Eventually it was hoped that they would get fed up and leave.

We once stayed the night with friends in the Dordogne. Their difficult neighbour across the valley had, so he claimed, a problem with *sanglier,* wild boar, eating his maize. In spite of the fact that no one else in the whole area had seen a boar, a cannon was employed. The noise was so loud and, being in a valley, reverberated against the hillside startling not only any *sanglier* but everyone else within miles. It also continued about every eight minutes throughout the night and we were very glad to get home. It is actually illegal to use a cannon after dark and eventually we were told that, in this case, the police were called in and dismantled it.

Raymond, having installed his machine somewhere in the middle of the vineyard, was concerned that it worked as it should. All was well for the first evening and we hadn't had any sightings of starlings that day. Raymond and Mike sat on the porch drinking an aperitif while I prepared supper listening to Beethoven's Second on *France Musique,* divinely played by an orchestra under Simon Rattle. Through the open door I could see the line of cows standing near the fence, watching Raymond and listening to his voice. The last few distant bangs of the cannon stopped as the light faded. Raymond drained his glass, bid us *'Bonne soirée'*, and we heard the tractor start up and then die away.

The next day, while we were preparing for our

guests, the cannon suddenly stopped in the afternoon and, having been mended, did not stop as dusk fell. There was nothing for it but to switch it off later by hand. Raymond was going to a reunion that night. Would we do it? Of course. But we forgot. By the time we remembered, it was very dark. We decided to drive up the edge of the vineyard in our old 2CV. We didn't want to risk our other car. The cannon is a small device, attached to a similarly sized gas cylinder. It sat on the ground somewhere about half way up one of the fifteen extremely long, leafy rows. I hopped out of the car while Mike turned it, trying to avoid the ditch. He parked and climbed out.

'Can you see it?'

'You have to be joking!'

'It's about two rows down from the *poteau*,' he called.

'I can't even see the bloody *poteau*,' I shouted. 'Wait. I'll get a torch.'

Anyone watching would have thought we were completely mad. We wandered up and down the vines with an ever more feeble torch in a darkness so deep that even the tall concrete electricity pole somewhere in the middle was invisible. The odd thing was that the noise, which should have guided us, was distorted and muffled in the thick leaves. Clearly the sound went straight upward for the benefit of the birds. Eventually Mike drove the 2CV across the ditch and around to the bottom of the vineyard and we advanced and reversed, sweeping each row with the main beam until we finally located the wretched thing. I walked up and switched off the cylinder. We bumped home down the uneven track, left the 2CV outside the barn and, at last, settled down for supper.

Chapter Fourteen

It was early evening. The last before our friends would arrive to stay. Mike had already swum and had gone to shower, fix an aperitif and write a letter to Matthew. I stripped off and swam nude, an extra delight and something I don't do when we have guests, not that I think they'd mind. The sun had been glorious all day with an intermittent gusty wind. I managed twenty lengths and each time I reached the deep end the perfume from the great rambling shrub by the pool was overwhelming. With its dull green leaves, silvered underneath, and the very small, hidden, creamy flowers, I wish my *elaeagnus ebbingei* had a more attractive common name. The 'bee bush' might do. At this time of the year the scent attracts bees of every kind. In the grand humming chorus of insects it seemed to be the smallest that made the most noise, apart from the occasional *bourdon,* the great black bumblebee. The perfume at the other end of this rural pool was not so appealing. Rotting fruit from two wild plum trees, which we had to cut back before we left, covered the rough ground.

We had spent the morning shopping and the afternoon making a huge *boeuf bourguignon.* The beds were ready, the sheets rough dried in the sun and the wind. I hauled myself out of the pool to sunbathe and had fortunately just wrapped myself in a towel when M. Carpentier *et fils,* armed with pickaxes, appeared unexpectedly. They would like to make a start on digging out the ground. Was that *convenable?* With guests due the following day it was, of course, highly inconvenient, but so anxious were we to see the work begun that we agreed. For the next couple of hours they hacked away, the space growing larger and larger. If it rained now, I thought, not only would our lake be twice the size, it would also be filled with mud. But, there being no sign of even a passing cloud, we hoped for the best. They were, at least, tidy workers. They continued until about seven-thirty, laid down planks for our guests to walk on and left with a promise to return at the weekend to concrete in the strong wooden support and cut the steps.

The next morning we were up early. *Les Spears,* as Raymond calls them, would already be disembarking from the train at Brive. The temperature on our porch was only 54 degrees, a reminder that it really was September, but the low sun was already fierce in a blue, blue sky. Still in shadow, the cows were putty coloured, the sun just catching their rumps as they moved in unhurried fashion across the field. Heavy dew on the electricity wire swung loops of silver across the distant fields; the tall *poteau* in the vineyard now clearly visible. The far hillside, still undefined, was grey with mist. All the plastic chairs were drenched and the morning glories, which are Mike's special favourites, lived up to their name, opening bold and bright against the rough white wall. Last year's pristine gravel path, now with a baby-fine green covering, glistening with moisture, clearly needed more weed-killer. There was no wind; hence perfect conditions for the job, but it was almost too beautiful to attack.

We have a young, self-sown peach tree at the corner of the *chai*. The fruit, *pêche de vigne,* are small with delicious, red-stained flesh. As its name implies this variety was grown at the end of rows of vines, whether, as with roses, to warn of disease, or just to refresh the pickers I'm not sure. This summer for the first time our little tree was heavy with peaches. Had the trunk been stronger the branch would have broken, as so often happens with Raymond's plum trees. As it was, the whole tree was leaning over. We were sure our guests would help solve the problem. *Les Spears* arrived about midday looking fragile.

Mary and Bernard are both over eighty and Mary, in particular, had not been well. Over the next few days they began to recover from the journey. Nan and Tony, our other guests who have been coming to Bel-Air for the last 25 years, arrived the next day and as Nan had once been a nurse this lent authority to our welcoming Mary strictly as convalescent. All she was allowed to do was pick some peaches.

Sunday was Mike's birthday. We had organised a cake and champagne for later that evening but were all summoned after lunch to take dessert at the farm. It was not one of Claudette's giant *baba au rhum,* a *tarte aux poires,* or *clafouti aux prunes,* but another birthday cake complete with candles and *Joyeux Anniversaire* in bright pink icing. There was a bottle of Armagnac for Mike and even a present for me as I had missed my French birthday celebrations in April of that year. Mary asked about the industrial-sized refrigerated cupboard humming away under the hanger. It was the first time our friends had seen it. Claudette smiled and once again told proudly about her solution to the problem of the regulations from Brussels.

'On *l'a acheté pour le petit veau, cette année,*' she said. She wasn't going to repeat the outrage of the previous year and lose all her special delicacies.

'Then who killed the calf?' asked Mary.

'It was cousin Robert, *l'ancien boucher,* who had

slaughtered the calf for us at the farm this spring,' she explained.

'He cut its throat,' she said, matter of factly. 'The proper way to kill an animal.'

She didn't approve of electrical stunning, claiming that it didn't always work. This method was quick and they had hung the carcass in the new fridge. Bernie was interested, saying that this was the way both Kosher and Halal animals are killed. I mused about the beautiful little calf, and also about Robert, who loves bees and all living creatures.

I had noticed that Raymond was wearing his striped jersey. Soon he disappeared and we heard him returning with the old Citroen. It stood gleaming and throbbing in the courtyard to be admired.

'C'est pour les Spears,' declared Raymond. 'On va faire un tour.'

Nan and Tony had already sampled the transformed car the previous year. Mary, always elegant, tied a scarf over her wide sun hat, making a perfect Edwardian lady, and off they went, waving regally. Cake and champagne were repeated at about nine o'clock that evening at Bel-Air.

'Deux fois, le champagne,' said Raymond happily raising his glass. 'C'était une bonne idée!'

Sleeping every afternoon under the tree, Mary continued to recover and, their brief stay soon over, they, like us, decided to drive all the way home. Soon they were packing up and looking at the map.

A single *sternbergia* appeared in the garden. I had first noticed these bright yellow, crocus-like flowers when we visited the hilltop town of Bellaye many years before, late in September. Bellaye looks down on a loop of the river Lot, giving a superb view of the surrounding Cahors vineyards. These brilliant flowers were everywhere, pushing up through the grass verges between short, pointed green leaves. I imagined them to be a yellow version of an autumn crocus but later I discovered that they were of the same family as daffodils and snowdrops and, rather to my surprise, hippeastrums. They originate in Greece where they can cover a hillside and are thought to be the 'lilies of the field' of the Bible. I had bought a few plants in the market one summer and as they are totally invisible for most of the year it is easy to forget exactly where they've been planted. They make an exotic contrast against another of my late flowering favourites, the *desmodium*. This is a shrub with long arching sprays of small, pea-like, dark pink flowers which sway in the wind. It dies away completely in the winter, leaving a tangle of dry stems which make good kindling. The new shoots are the only problem. They push through the grass and weeds in late spring, just when I am busy with the strimmer. I have made many a mistake. It is so infuriating to think that the two-inch shoot, a bit like a coltsfoot, that I have just cut off, would, in a couple of months, had I been less clumsy, have become a flowering delight, four feet long.

It was gardening weather. Cyclamen, which Tony planted years ago, appeared under the rose bushes. Nancy bought more in the market and dug them in around the trunk of the ash tree. We cut back the japonica and pruned the early roses. We borrowed Raymond's long tree lopper to tackle the laurels. Not for Raymond a modern aluminium version as I have in London. His was made with a long straight branch cut from the wood. The blades were fixed at the top somewhat precariously with a single nail and were manipulated by pulling on a rope. It was not easy. We took turns. We had planted the laurels behind the low wall which shelters the pool from the north. They were growing ever taller and wider. Mike insisted that they were completely out of hand. I rather enjoyed their profusion. As usual it was Nan who arbitrated and then did most of the work. While I did my best with the side facing the pool, she took more drastic measures on the other side.

It was just as well we made the most of the weather. The next afternoon the sun disappeared. There was a change in the air. Ominous clouds began to loom up from the west and we could hear distant thunder. We can see for many miles and watched the storm approaching. There seemed to be two dark funnels but it was all moving very slowly. We made tea and sat up high on the terrace for a ringside view. The thunder rolled around for an hour and a half, like an angry bull, uncertain whether or not to strike. There was a brief reappearance of the sun, perhaps it would miss us after all, but a spattering of rain eventually made us pack up the tea. As we did so there was sudden, brilliant, sheet lightning. We hurried under the porch, thunder deafening us right overhead. For about three minutes we watched as a heavy downpour raced and gurgled down the water channel but then we had to dive for cover. Hailstones, larger than cherries, came horizontally across the field and clattered onto the porch. In seconds they had built into a pile around the base of the well and even skittered through the open door into the house. The noise was furious. We ran into the green room, which Nan and Tony were using, and which faced the storm, to see water cascading down the north-facing wall. The hail-stones, so fierce and at such an angle, had simply forced themselves up under the tiles. There was already a leak above the bed. Nan and I simply rolled up the whole mattress and bedding and rushed it through the front door, across the living room and into the yellow bedroom. We laughed as there were already two mattresses on this bed. Now there would be three. The story of the Princess and the pea came to mind. It was just as well they changed their bedroom as the excavation outside their door was now indeed a very large muddy lake.

It all stopped as suddenly as it had started and the next morning the sun shone, the sky was blue once more and *les Carpentiers* appeared early and cut a drainage channel. The water vanished and the earth steamed. They brought up the handsome, square wooden support for the new roof section. It had a metal peg at the base, which they hammered and then cemented into place, and the next day they fixed the sloping diagonal cross beam of the new roof and the two straight edges at right angles which were cemented into each wall. Now we could see how it would all work. These timbers were untreated and Tony and Mike spent most of the day with brushes and a tin of wood preservative. Soon our old friends, so much a part of Bel-Air, had to leave for their long journey back to Northumberland and were not able to see that corner of the house finished. 'A *l'année prochaine,*' we toasted. Next year!

There were minor crises during the next few days when the cement mixer broke down and young Carpentier who was, we learnt, called Peter – pronounced *Pitaire* – had to mix by hand. Eventually our wide steps were cemented and by the end of the week, when his father came to inspect the work, there was only the roof to be finished. We left M. Carpentier fixing the rafters and went to buy *voliges,* the laths to go underneath the tiles. These were already treated with a lurid yellow preservative and it was quite a relief when they were covered. Our pile of ancient tiles from the Château were unearthed and carefully overlapped. Our perennial problem had finally been solved, the umbrella could be moved from the bedroom door, and guests in the green room would not now get wet before they reached the shower.

The storm had cleared the air. The weather was gentle. Misty mornings were followed by golden days, droning with harvests. Our view across the fields was once again revealed, chunk by chunk, as a great green combine lowered its silver rockets and carved its way through Raymond's wide field of maize, five rows at a time. Usually it is a steady stream of corn-cobs, which hurtle out into the waiting trailer. They then go to be dried all winter long in the high wire cages, *les cribs,* which stride so decoratively across the countryside. This time it was different. I watched as the combine spilt out single grains, like silage, but a larger stream and pure gold, unlike the variations from lime green to ash brown of silage. Jean-Michel came by briefly, keeping an eye on the proceedings.

'*On va faire la farine, cet après-midi,*' he shouted. 'You should come and have a look.'

All was creamy white flour in the barn when we went down after lunch to watch the milling. Jean-Michel, his eyebrows and hair already coated, as were his long cotton coat and Wellingtons, looked like a snowman, or a street mime artist, except that he was never still. He was clearly in charge, with Raymond nowhere to be seen. I knew that there was an old, battered milling machine in the other barn, rather like an extra large baby mouli. This was clearly a much more sophisticated arrangement. The tractor, with its small but powerful mill attachment, had been backed into the barn. The golden grain poured in and the flour flowed out of a tube into a trough lined with black plastic. Jean-Michel, in between yelling instructions, was tramping it down and levelling it off. The head of the farming machine cooperative, to which Raymond belongs, had brought a small group of interested students. They took turns to drive the trailer back for fresh supplies. No dubious animal protein or other undesirables would be going into this winter feed.

Everything was turning colour. Our sumach trees are always the first to come into their true glory, followed by the Virginia creeper. Even the leaves on the *boule de neige* were tipped with pink. We had seven fat, glowing, pinkish-red pomegranates hanging outside the living room window. Across the newly cut maize field I could see the glowing shape of a field of soya bean. Close up one can distinguish the wonderful tones of yellow, orange and scarlet. Scarlet too were strings of berries twined round the barn door by the white bryony, which, with a root like an enormous white swede, rampages everywhere with its delicately shaped leaves. Even the leaves on the fig tree were turning. Some of the remaining fruit, too high to reach, had split open and peeled back showing the soft, red-brown flesh and golden seeds. The last few peaches hung on our little tree. On our way to buy wine to take home from the *Coopérative* we passed a splendid field of millet. The ripened spears of bronze glowed in the sunlight against an almost violet sky. I thought of our friend Jean, a painter, who was coming back to her house and studio in the village in a few days' time. Jean had recently retired from running a busy art department and was, I knew, looking forward to her new freedom to stay and enjoy the autumn landscape. But she would have to hurry. The drone of distant combines signalled a complete change of scene. Two days later the burnished rows of millet had vanished, replaced by great brown furrows of rich soil.

We made our last trip to the market at Libos, the road winding through contrasting colours of newly turned fields; some white with chalk, others red with iron, and every shade of brown in-between. The market was full of anoraks and parkas, warm slippers, woolly hats and padded gloves, pumpkins and *pruneaux* and hunting gear. The herb and spice stall is always in the same place but you could find it anyway by following your nose. I bought a large bag of verveine for making tisane; my own little plant, whose leaves I used to dry in the sun, had not survived last year's frosts. *Herbes de Provence* were also on my list and, this year, *baies roses,* the bright red berry which colours the selection of mixed peppers. I first tasted them in a restaurant in Agen, where we ate swordfish *au baies roses.* The tiny peppercorns had a unique, aromatic flavour, and were so delicious I wanted to repeat the experience. The name simply translates as pink berries, which is not helpful. The spice man told me that it is not actually a peppercorn at all, but a berry from a tree. He did not know the correct name and neither do I, yet.

On Saturday the first grapes would be picked. We always stay to help with the first *vendange,* which is in an old sloping vineyard, the vines planted closer together, before harvesting with machines was thought of. It was a beautiful morning, the air fresh and the sun soon strong enough to encourage a row of cardigans and jackets draped along the vines. Raymond drove the tractor, pulling the small trailer into which strong young men emptied our baskets, heavy with grapes. These were, in their turn, tipped into a large trailer which, at the end of the day, would wind its way slowly behind the winking light of the tractor, to the *Cave Coopérative.* There was, alas, no Madame Barrou this morning.

'*Elle a la sciatique,*' said Raymond dolefully. Everyone sympathised.

As requested, I left the vineyard and went down to the farm at about eleven-fifteen to help cut the bread, stir the soup, wash the salad, cut the tart, filter the *rosé,* lay the table, and put out basins of hot water and bars of yellow soap for *les vendangeurs* to wash their hands. However, apart from the soap and water, Claudette – with her usual efficiency – had already done most of it. I washed up a couple of saucepans and we sat chatting in a rare moment of nothing to do, until the first cars turned into the courtyard and weary workers climbed out stiffly, stretched their backs, washed their hands and sniffed in happy anticipation the good smells coming from the kitchen.

We were seventeen at the long table under the hangar, six English, including Kevin, still hard at work on the chateau, his wife and children, two friends, and two Portugese. As we drained our homemade aperitifs and lifted the lids on the great soup tureens, the talk was of the authorities, who were getting more vigilant. Every addition or improvement to one's property was being monitored they agreed, as they ladled out the soup. I remembered an occasion, long ago, when this very hangar was in the first stages of being spruced up. We had gone down one morning to find Raymond and Claudette busy moving furniture. There was, we learnt, a rumour of an impending visit to the whole village by some rating official. We were swiftly coopted into transforming the hangar back into being *'non habitable'*. Old sacks were hung over the new radiators. Chairs and tables were removed. Old baskets and implements were hung about and a rack of onions pushed against the wall. Finally the oldest 2CV was driven up over the newly paved floor which was scattered with earth. It was all done with speed and much glee. Whether the official ever came or not I don't remember.

Now they talked of people in Provence who were, it was rumoured, erecting plastic screens to foil the official helicopters who made regular inspections, taking aerial photographs of new pools and extensions.

'They measure everything,' said Jean-Michel, darkly.

For once Raymond agreed with him. 'You remember the cotton you found, Ruth?' he laughed.

Some weeks before I had returned from shopping and, having parked the car, had idly wound up a length of thread lying at the edge of the field. I wondered at first if it had come from the hem of a skirt until it grew ever longer. It was Raymond who solved the mystery when he mentioned that the official who spends his days walking round the fields with his cotton measure had recently been.

'But they must use up hundreds of kilometres of thread?' I had said.

'Bien sur,' Raymond replied 'But – you can say your

field is so many *hectares,* they don't necessarily believe you, *les bureaucrates*!'

Soup finished, he poured the wine. The soup was followed by two, beautifully arranged, *plateaux* of hors-d'oeuvre: eggs with bright gold yolks, large field tomatoes, a mound of fish in mayonnaise. They were soon demolished. People had been working since eight-thirty with, as usual, no mid-morning break. Next we had a dish of cauliflower, cooked, drained and chopped up very small. Tiny shreds of bacon were added and the mixture had been baked in a thick and tasty *béchamel.* The pace of eating grew slower as slices of roast pork were served. These were followed by green salad, cheese and, finally, *tarte aux poires.* The children ran about in the courtyard as Claudette poured coffee into our wine glasses. This was a working lunch. No elegant coffee cups from Limoges today. Conversation rolled round the table. Raymond's brother was in fine form. He is older than Raymond and has bright twinkling eyes.

'Ah, we're all getting older,' he said. There was no denying that!

'You know what we're called?' he asked me.

'*Le troisième âge,*' I said.

'*Oh ça, oui,*' he shrugged. Then he smiled. '*Mais aussi, les Tamalous.*'

'*Les Tamalous?*' I'd never heard this expression. It sounded vaguely oriental.

'*Oui*,' he said triumphantly, '*Les Tamalous!*'

'*Mais pourquoi?*'

'*Parce que*,' he spoke slowly. '*Maintenant, quand on se rencontre, on dit toujours, "T'as mal, ou?"*'

Every time we meet each other nowadays, we say: 'You've got an ache? Where is it?'

CHAPTER FIFTEEN

Three days before we leave and the wisteria, the clematis and the bignonia have still to be cut back, the oleander in its pot must be moved to the south-facing terrace. All the other tender plants must be loaded into Raymond's old *fourgonnette* and taken down to their winter quarters where Claudette will care for them until the spring. It was Jean-Michel who, several years ago, endeared himself to his new mother-in-law, or in the much more gallant French version, his *belle-mère*, by constructing large, wooden-framed, plastic screens with which, in winter, she could close in the open-ended hangar, to make it frostproof.

M. Escoffier will come to close our pool the day after tomorrow, which means we can swim up to the last minute. Gone are the days when we spent hours hauling out the ladder, adding the winter product to keep the water clean and prevent its freezing, and wrestling with the heavy winter cover. This was an earlier primitive cover weighted down round the edge with six or eight long inner tubes. Strings were attached to the tubes so that they could be threaded through the cover, hauled into place and then filled with water. The whole procedure would take us the best part of a very wet day.

I check the cupboards. Nothing must be left anywhere that is within reach of mice. Everything remotely edible must be put in tins for if they are especially hungry they will chew through strong plastic boxes. One year, large holes were gnawed in the outlet hose on the washing machine and there were teeth marks on what was left of an old bar of Wright's coal-tar soap! I make a list in my notebook *'pour la prochaine fois,'* for next time. I find it impossible to remember when I am in London exactly how much dark brown sugar, mixed spice, Earl Grey tea or jars of mincemeat I have left. There are few things now that one cannot buy in France, even Marmite and peanut butter, which were always on the list for the children in the early days. But of course some are more expensive. Tea we bring from England and I always make sure that we return with enough coffee to last us through the winter. Mike takes care of the wine.

The washing machine trundles away on its last load in our outside laundry, where, long ago, my predecessor Anaïs kept her pig. I stow the sun-aired bedding in wooden chests scented with lavender and close the rooms one by one. Who will be sleeping in them next year? We have many regular visitors but we also enjoy seeing friends who sometimes break their journey by spending a few days at Bel-Air. In the children's room there are bits of Lego under the bed, a single sock. Two somewhat lonely garden chairs remain by the pool, the rest are carried in and stacked. There is a certain satisfaction about thinking: that's the last time I need to wash that pot, shake that rug, sweep that floor, but, in weather like this, it seems madness deliberately to return to cold and damp, to city crowds and an inevitably more stressful lifestyle.

Our friends from Spain will arrive this evening. It is not good timing for us but they are en route to visit relations in Brussels and will, in any case, sleep at the farm. We have taken Raymond and Claudette to stay with them several times in La Guardia, an ancient hill-top town in Northern Spain, surrounded by the vineyards of La Rioja, and Claudette is anxious to return their hospitality. I make a tart with a box of blackcurrants I find at the back of the freezer compartment and take down the last of the ice cream. Mike is a French ice cream addict and there is a much greater variety of flavours than in England. Seriously dark chocolate is his favourite.

Our friends arrive safely and the next morning

Mariá Arrate insists on going to market in Villeneuve. Having brought us all peppers, *chorizo,* paprika, jam, and honey from her bees, Mariá Arrate, an intrepid shopper, is now buying cheese and pâté and beetroot to take to her brother. Pâté to Brussels seems rather like coals to Newcastle to me but she is unstoppable. We intended to have a simple lunch in the garden and bought *crevettes,* bread and salad in the market, but Claudette insists that we eat *ensemble.* We take down our meagre contribution and begin with the last of our local melons, and one brought from Spain, Raymond grudgingly admitting that the Spanish variety has a certain merit. We share out our prawns and continue with slices of veal, and a sauce made with tiny mushrooms and olives. Next we sample the vegetable, which Mariá has also brought with her. She and Claudette had already set about cooking it. It is called *Bourache,* which translates as borage, and we only eat the stems. After five minutes in the pressure cooker with slices of onion, pumpkin and salt it is served. I find it edible but unremarkable. Mariá mashes hers up with olive oil.

Claudette reminds me that, before we leave, I must pick a hundred leaves from my little peach tree if I want to make *vin de pêche,* the delicious aperitif we have just enjoyed. I had always imagined it was with the fruit that this was made but now I learn that I must marinade my leaves in *eau de vie* for two months then add one glass of the strained liquid to each litre of medium sweet white wine.

'*Mais, pas trop doux,*' advises Claudette. 'It's best to taste and add sugar if necessary.'

Mariá Arrate and her husband José Mari, are taken on a tour of the farm and then to *France Prune,* the Co-operative where the local plums are finally taken. They always stock up with *les Pruneaux d'Agen,* for all their friends and family, when they are here. We return to Bel-Air for our final preparations.

I cut the last of the lavender and the Chinese lanterns. The lanterns I hang outside in the porch to make the house look less forlorn when we leave. The lavender is tied upside down in paper bags and hung from the giant nail in the corridor. This is where Anaïs, so Grandma told me, always hung her tansy, her verveine and other herbs to dry. Next spring I shall strip the stems and add to my lavender bags. I cut back the bignonia, my red trumpet climber, which fell off the wall in a high wind two years ago. It was bent over at such an acute angle I feared that it might die but new shoots are already up to the roof while the fallen trunk makes a spectacular hedge of flowers.

I do my best with the fragile stems of the clematis, twisted up into the wisteria which, once again, reaches out its tendrils to lasso anything within reach. I am not much good at cutting back; much better at planting.

Back to the farm at eight o'clock yet again to eat together, we begin with *le tourin*, the famous, extremely garlicky soup with which newly weds, and others, are sometimes surprised in the middle of the night. Then Claudette has made *crêpes* filled with *jambon de York* and cheese. These are followed by her own *confit de canard*, a gigantic mushroom omelette and slices of her home-cured ham. I am amused to realise that we have eaten ham and eggs twice in the same meal; not one of Claudette's most inspired choices of menu. However, she has been out with her guests most of the afternoon and has still managed to whip up an upside-down cake with pears, which she serves with a hot chocolate sauce. After coffee, and the obligatory *pruneau* in *eau de vie* in our still-warm cups, the best porcelain from Limoges this time, we bid farewell to the Spaniards. They will be en route for Brussels early the next morning and we shall be in the final throes of packing. They are trying hard to persuade Raymond and Claudette to go back with them to Spain when they make the return journey in a few days' time. Raymond is clearly eager for an impromptu holiday but Claudette will take more time to decide.

The next morning is another cloudless golden day. We force ourselves to load the car. I carry everything onto the porch; Mike does the loading. Having been, as an eighteen-year-old, part of a tank crew, he is still an expert at packing a small space. We seem to have a great many cases of wine, but I say nothing. I feel less guilty about my files, my boxes of books, piles of clothes bought in *la friperie,* and umpteen jars of strawberry jam for my kind neighbour who waters my plants in London. At last it is finished. The car is full, apart from a gap at the back, which we know from past experience that we must leave for Claudette to fill.

We have a last swim. I lie basking in the water while, miles above me, a tiny silver plane moves, with the faintest of sounds, towards Bordeaux, leaving a soft white trail across the blue expanse. Later, as we sit enjoying our favourite view for the last time this summer, a solitary cat walks up the track as if we have already gone. She passes the house and disappears in the stubble to go hunting. It is very still. We rest, lost in thought, until we see M. Escoffier's white van coming quietly up the track. We wait to greet him, pick up the last two chairs and go indoors as the evening bell sounds across the fields.

The house already looks strange. Furniture, which normally lives outside, is stacked in corners. The sofa and armchairs are covered in plastic sheets. Everything is ready now to leave in the morning. Last minute turning off the water, stripping the bed and securing the shutters will take an hour. We get dressed in tomorrow's travelling clothes, and take all the edible bits and pieces from the fridge down to the farm. The inedible are also taken for the pigs: forgotten potatoes (already sprouting), limp salad, and old bread, hard as wood.

Claudette is stirring the soup, Raymond has opened a very dusty bottle, something that smells delicious is sizzling in a covered pan. This kitchen is a special place to us. For 25 years we, and so many of our friends, have been welcomed here without ceremony. We have eaten grand banquets off the best china with the extended family. Food fit for kings, meals that started at midday and went on till five o'clock in the afternoon. Mike and I have also, after returning from some trip together, eaten simple leftovers, after Claudette has scurried round to shut up the baby ducklings while I lay the table and wash the salad and Mike goes off to the *cave* with Raymond. We know we have been very privileged.

The following morning, ready to leave at last, Mike locks the door with the large key, its once attached, tattered shred of red cloth long vanished and replaced with string. One peach remains and as I take it I suddenly remember. Mike sits, fairly patiently, in the car while I pick one hundred leaves as fast as I can. We take a long, last look at Bel-Air for this year. We so nearly didn't get here. Although still too thin, and not as completely back to normal as he would wish, my husband is more relaxed, bronzed and fitter. It has been a good summer. And as well as restoring our health and spirits, we have also managed to solve our last real headache with the house. The new corner, roofed over with the ancient tiles from the Château, blends in so well it might always have been there. We drive down to the farm to leave the keys. Waiting for us on the table under the hangar are a *plateau* of grapes picked early that morning, a box of eggs, *confit de canard* to put in the cold box and a jar of prunes in *eau de vie*. There is just enough room. After a last cup of coffee, hugs and kisses and promises to write, we circle the courtyard still bright with flowers, a wave and we are en route.

The inevitable sadness of leaving is mitigated by the prospect of staying the next night in the ancient city of Bourges, where we have booked a room. The receptionist has assured me that the hotel is well within walking distance of the great cathedral, which, I have read, holds some of the most wonderful stained glass in the whole of France. It is always difficult to adjust to staying the first night in a city after so many weeks surrounded by open countryside and I am slightly claustrophobic. We find our hotel in Bourges, but our proposed room is in a gloomy, modern annexe. The Hotel des Tilleuls is not, by any stretch of the imagination, anywhere near the centre of the city. We take another brief look at the room and turn it down, rather like the corners of the mouth of the astonished receptionist.

Now to find another hotel – not easy. All 86 rooms in the Hôtel Ibis are taken. An elderly local driver throws up his hands as the *navigateur* tries to help the driver to negotiate the one-way system in what is, by now, rush hour in Bourges. Twice more we draw a blank. Mike is surprisingly calm but I know it won't last. The next hotel kindly gives us a map and a recommendation. When we eventually find the Hotel d'Angleterre it seems almost forgotten, sitting quietly at the corner of a square with a tinkling fountain. We are in luck this time. Not only do they have a lovely room and charming staff, but also a drive-in garage, a consideration when the car is so loaded. The manager sighs and explains that for some inexplicable reason, although they are in the oldest and loveliest part of Bourges, they are not in this year's Michelin guide. We commiserate but are secretly thankful.

We get the last table for dinner that evening at the nearby restaurant, the Hostellerie de Jacques Coeur, where a large number of black-coated waiters serve with silent expertise. Our *crottin de chèvre chaud* – a small, warmed goat's cheese – on its bed of crisp lettuce is placed reverently before us. My pigeon is delicious, Mike's steak less so, but there are no vegetables. We finish with hot chocolate pudding with a runny centre, served with mint ice cream. We only drink a glass of rosé each and, for France, the meal is expensive, but it is just the kind of soothing that we need after a long drive.

The next morning we get our first glimpse of the Cathedral Sainte-Etienne. It takes a moment after stepping through the door to realise that the amazing effect of the sheer length of the great nave is partly due to there being no transepts to break the line. The whole space is flooded with shafts of coloured light. The morning sun streams in through windows on every level, the lowest in the side chapels, double windows down the length of the aisles and great high windows almost to the vaulted roof, and colour and pattern everywhere. The cathedral was an ambitious project when it was begun in 1190, and the interior of the nave with its four aisles was not completed until 1270.

The earliest and most precious windows are at the far end, in the rounded cloister, and were removed during the war for safekeeping. We just sit and gaze in wonder. The themes for these windows are thought to have been chosen by one Guillaume de Bourges, Archbishop until 1209 and later canonised. Formerly a Cistercian monk, he was said to favour meditation and reflection and this part of the cathedral is where the earliest worship was held. The designs are so clear; no need for binoculars, or craning necks. These are the illustrated catechisms of their time and were intended to be studied from close up. Themes from the old and new testaments are juxtaposed. There are depictions of the parables of Jesus; the Prodigal Son, looking somewhat apprehensive at leaving home, and the Good Samaritan, and also the stories of the Apocalypse and the Last Judgement.

As so many undoubtedly have done for hundreds of years before us, we marvel at this vivid medieval glass, fashioned by the master craftsmen who also worked at Chartres. Other local craftsmen, who, at the time, contributed money for the great enterprise, are also commemorated. While Joseph lies, head on hand, perhaps contemplating the Pharaoh's dream of seven fat and seven lean cattle, in the windows beneath him the medieval cooper, carpenter, and wheel-wright, busy at their work, are remembered.

Almost opposite our hotel is the fifteenth-century palace of Jacques Coeur, the Superintendant of Finance to King Charles VII. It is clearly a fascinating building and we begin a brief tour but are still so stunned with the beauty of the cathedral we feel we cannot do it justice. We leave, promising ourselves another visit to Bourges, another year. The road from Bourges to Sancerre is a delight, a patchwork of vines ready for harvest. The motorway up to the east of Paris is a different story. My days of enjoying fast motorway travelling are over and Mike finds his eyes are becoming very tired. We are glad to reach Compiègne. Alas, Compiègne seems as full as Bourges had been the previous night and this time there is no quiet, forgotten hotel with a tinkling fountain. We drive on to Noyon, fearing to find the same problem and deciding that we have reached an age when it might be more prudent and less stressful to pre-book. We are lucky. The Hotel Saint-Eloi, with its *Restaurant Gastronomique,* sounds promising. We are not disappointed. The wonderfully extravagant mid-nineteenth-century house, complete with a grand ballroom, has only been a hotel for the last hundred years. It must have been originally designed for someone extremely wealthy and very elegant. Our room is very comfortable and the chef superb.

We feast on delicate, sliced *noisettes* of lamb with tiny vegetables all encased in a shell of the finest puff pastry. The desserts are shaped like boats, creations filled with variously flavoured creams and with sails of spun sugar, some of caramel, others of bitter chocolate. They are almost too beautiful to eat but once started, irresistible. The whole bill, including room and breakfast, comes to 145 Euros. As they say in the guide books, 'worth a detour.'

It seems a fitting end to our summer in France.

CHAPTER SIXTEEN

Through the dark days of winter we looked forward to a visit to Bel-Air the following spring. It seemed a long time since we had been able to watch our trees come into leaf, to enjoy the plum blossom in the orchards, wild jonquils in the meadow and go for long walks in the fresh, sweet air. In spite of inevitably chilly mornings and evenings of that season and the constant cutting of wood to replenish the fire, we love the sun-filled few weeks we usually have in the early part of the year. It was made especially nostalgic for me as I showed early slides of Bel-Air each time I was invited to do one of my lectures about my books.

But Mike was not well. Although there was no return of the cancer, the damage done to surrounding nerves during what had been an extensive operation, and his perpetual anxiety about this, was affecting us both. To balance his unhappiness I found myself assuming a relentlessly cheerful role. The after-care at St George's Hospital was conscientious but limited. The urologist was noncommittal. Sister Ho, in charge of the colorectal unit, was always ready to listen and advise but Mike was keenly aware that his own anxiety was part of the problem and also that, every day, both she and the consultants had to deal with another dozen frightened patients still awaiting surgery. He was supposed to be one of the fortunate ones. The successful removal of a cataract at Moorfields Eye Hospital at the end of February diverted him but, in April, instead of our hoped-for trip to France, he had to return to St George's for a hernia operation. Then, after he had some pain in his chest, slight angina was diagnosed and medication prescribed. Next year, we promised ourselves, we will make it in the spring.

We rang Raymond, only to learn with some surprise from Claudette that he and Corinne, Philippe's wife, were stuck in Milan. What on earth were they doing there? They had been invited to Jordan, explained Claudette, to stay with Marie-Jo, Raymond's niece and godchild. Marie-Jo's husband, who worked for France Telecom, was in charge of setting up a new system in Jordan. It was a real opportunity, agreed Claudette, whose motto is usually *'il faut en profiter'* but, at the last minute, Corinne had gone with Raymond, as Claudette had become too fearful of the international situation. *'J'avais peur,'* Claudette admitted. Now the two travellers were stranded overnight in Italy because there were twenty centimetres of snow in Jordan! Until the shocked authorities could get to grips with this unheard-of phenomenon, no planes were landing. It was the beginning of a year of disturbed and destructive weather.

With Mike once more home from hospital, and making a good recovery, we made plans to leave London early in July. In May, Sally phoned to ask if we would consider letting Bel-Air to a friend who was in the process of moving to live in France. She, her husband and small boy had rented – or so they thought – a house for a month while they finished making their own house habitable. They were expecting a baby in August, the rented house had been double-booked and they had nowhere to go. We agreed. At least she could water my plants, I thought.

I need not have worried about drought. On the night of June 4th a hurricane with winds of up to a hundred miles an hour raged across the north of Lot-et-Garonne. Forty millimetres of rain fell in two hours and hail battered the countryside. I had a frantic phone call about nine o'clock that evening from a very frightened young woman at Bel-Air, asking me what to do as there was water pouring in everywhere. Though sympathetic and naturally concerned, there wasn't much I could do from Clapham except advise her to use every available bucket and saucepan. We were accustomed to sudden storms but this one was clearly exceptional. We later heard about the firemen who worked through the night clearing fallen trees from the roads, the roofs blown clean away, and the orchards and vineyards devastated. She phoned again the next morning in a calmer mood to say that it had rained again that morning, normal rain this time, and none had come in. She had also realised how lucky they had been compared with their neighbours. 180 of Raymond's trees had been affected. Some could be hauled up into place again but many were simply cut in half. There were mudslides everywhere and the fields of maize and sunflowers were a sorry sight. When we phoned Raymond he was very dejected

'*En quelques minutes, des années de travail anéanties,*' he said. 'Years of work just wiped out.'

It seemed churlish to even wonder what state our garden would be in.

We had many calls and emails from our tenant. One morning she rang to say that the chimney sweep had just swept the chimney. He was demanding 100 euros and she hadn't enough to pay him. I forbore to ask her why she had let him in, in the first place, and spoke to this mysterious *ramoneur* myself. He sounded flustered and immediately reduced the price to eighty euros. I pointed out that as I hadn't ordered the chimney swept, and as there were several houses called Bel-Air in the region, it was likely that he had made a mistake. Perhaps he could return in a few weeks' time and we could discuss it. When I rang Raymond that evening he said, *'C'était un charlatan, sans doute,'* which was not exactly reassuring. The word went round the village and everyone was on the lookout for the charlatan but no one ever saw him again. A very small heap of soot lay in the garden to remind us of his passing.

Three weeks before we were due to leave Mike developed a rash. It was all over his body and very itchy. His GP was on holiday and the locum, diagnosing an allergy, prescribed a steroid cream. This made no difference. The rash began to turn into small blisters, which grew ever larger. He had a routine appointment at the cardiac clinic on a morning when I was unable to go with him as I was giving a talk. Very worried, I left him with instructions not to come home until he had seen a consultant. It took him all morning and a change of receptionist to finally get through the bureaucracy of the N.H.S. to see the cardiac consultant who, unsympathetic at first, changed his mind immediately when he saw the condition of Mike's skin. We saw the dermatologist that same afternoon.

She recognised the symptoms straight away and, within ten minutes, her diagnosis was confirmed by the consultant. Mike had developed *Bullous pemphigoid*, a serious disease of the auto-immune system in which one layer of the skin attacks the layer underneath. We were naturally anxious to know what had caused it. She said that it was not an allergy. Was it caused by stress? She did not think so, but, she admitted, neither was the cause really understood.

'But we're off to France next week,' said Mike.

'I'm afraid you'll have to postpone your visit for at least two weeks,' was the answer.

Mike fretted at the thought of yet another stay in hospital, but some of the blisters were by now as large as eggs, especially on the soles of his feet. As usual he coped with the illness with fortitude and a determination to learn as much as he could about it. A very high dose of steroids and an immune suppressant were prescribed and his progress monitored. He also had to take another preparation to line his stomach against all this medication. The treatment began to work. The blisters were drained and left dull red marks, which gradually faded. Eventually we were told he could leave hospital. Armed with a long list of his medication, letters for a dermatologist in France, strict instructions about blood tests to check for infection, and a gradual reduction of the steroid dose, we came home. Mike couldn't wait to get to Bel-Air and neither could I. Matthew helped us to pack and he loaded the car. We were off at last!

Down to Folkestone and through the tunnel, losing our way yet again trying to find the motor rail terminus and commiserating with other similarly lost travellers, I did not realise that Mike had deliberately cut down on his eating and – more importantly – his drinking, in order not to be inconvenienced on the overnight train journey. We slept well. At breakfast next morning in the station buffet, Mike drank a small coffee and had a glass of water with which to down his dozen different pills which he took all at once. We set off from Brive in high spirits, only eighty miles to go and we would be home.

After about half an hour, and fortunately on the smaller road, I began to notice that my husband was not in full control of the car. Alarmed, I begged him to stop. He was very reluctant, clearly concentrating hard, but his driving became more and more erratic. He sped up, then slowed and at every bend the car wandered across the road. It was not yet seven o'clock and thankfully there was almost no traffic. As by now I was almost in tears, he was at last persuaded and we pulled up at the side of the road. He got out and disappeared into the bushes. Should I take over the driving? When we are in France, apart from short shopping trips, Mike always drives, I navigate. Consequently, I am not too confident on long journeys. I cursed myself for allowing this situation to develop. When he reappeared he sat firmly in the driving seat and just fell asleep.

He slept for about twenty minutes and when he

woke seemed perfectly recovered. It was as though it had never happened. We set off again, my heart lurching at every bend, but he was his old confident self. We shopped briefly at Belves at a convenient supermarket close to the road, and soon we saw the outline of the church of Monflanquin on the horizon. Within half an hour we were turning into the familiar courtyard. We commiserated with Raymond and Claudette about the storm damage. Raymond nodded sadly. Claudette seemed more concerned with the fact that it was such a shame that we had not come earlier as they were all going to a concert that evening in a nearby church. The son of one of her cousins was giving a piano recital. Vincent is a brilliant young student and we would have much enjoyed hearing him but there was no way, after our journey, that we could even contemplate going.

'We'll all eat at seven,' said Claudette, giving us our keys. 'Then you can see how you feel.' She is ever-optimistic.

As we drove up the track, through Véronique's farm, the other track being still impassable, we could see the signs of devastation all around. A great swathe had been cut through the orchard. Trees, heavy with plums, lay prone. Bel-Air seemed to have been relatively lucky. The roof was intact and apart from several large branches from the ash tree, which had been hurled into the garden, and mud and leaves in the water channel, everything else seemed normal. There were even some roses blooming through the weeds. Once again, Susan had cleaned the house. We were home and safe. I could begin to unknot my still-tense stomach.

We heard more about the storm as we ate together later. What a beautiful evening it had been with absolutely no warning of what was to come. How it had raged for two hours.

'The area has been declared a disaster,' said Raymond. 'We'll get some compensation but,' he shrugged, 'new trees take six years before we get any profit.' As we waved them off to the concert he shouted, 'Oh, I forgot to tell you, your phone is not working. I've notified them.'

As I lay in bed that night, listening to the silence before finally drifting off to sleep, I resolved to insist on sharing the driving down in future and wondered whether I was, in fact, capable of doing so. I was so happy to be here and knew that it would take several days of the special peace and quiet we find at Bel-Air to recover from my fright on the journey. But at about midnight I was woken by Mike in a state of great anxiety.

'I've got cramp all over my body, every muscle,' he declared, wild-eyed. 'If it gets up to my heart I shall die!' I tried reasoning but to no avail. I had never seen him like this. He was literally shaking with fear. It was then I remembered that the phone was not working.

Véronique and Jean-Michel were away. Raymond and Claudette out. I would have to drive down to the village and wake someone up, Jean perhaps, but I wasn't even sure that she had arrived. Madame Barrou? But could I leave him in this state? My own heart was thumping as I tried to find some clothes. I heard a car coming up our track. Who could it be? I ran to the bedroom door and pulled it open. Too late – they had gone by. Then I saw the taillights and realised that the car had stopped further down the track by the water hydrant. A figure got out. It could only be Raymond who would stop there to check the water. They had obviously returned the back way from the concert in order to do just that. It seemed like a miracle. Still in my nightdress I ran through the long rough grass and down the track calling his name.

Within seconds he had come to Mike's aid. Clearly worried, he tried to calm him. Then Claudette stayed with me while Raymond returned to the farm to phone the doctor. When Dr Rouquié arrived he diagnosed acute dehydration and exhaustion. Dr Rouquié is also the deputy mayor of Monflanquin, and a solid, very reassuring figure. He stayed while Raymond went to knock up the duty pharmacist in Monflanquin and returned with yet more medication. Dr Rouquié discussed the steroid treatment and made an appointment for a blood test the following week, gave me a bill for forty pounds for a night call over a certain distance, and Raymond stayed till two a.m. What a tower of strength he was. When I finally got to bed I felt as though I had been through the Hundred Years War.

The next evening Judith was due to arrive. Mike absolutely insisted on driving to Agen to meet her. The high dose of steroids was weakening his muscles and he was determined to fight it. The weather was extremely hot. We were not to know that we were to experience the hottest summer on record. Jean came up to swim and sat drawing by the pool but the heat was just too intense to stay out of doors for long. Everyone was suffering. It was 100 degrees under our north-facing porch. Raymond said that no one could work after eleven in the morning. He came up twice a day to see how Mike was. Claudette sent melons and lettuces.

One morning Mike had a fever and I had to call the doctor out again. This time it was a throat infection, easily caught as he had almost no immune system. Another medication was added to the list and I made a chart and doled out the pills and capsules at intervals, ticking them off as I did so. The weather grew steadily hotter. I never thought that I would dread the sun coming up but the air just didn't cool down at night as it usually did. There was absolutely no breeze and each sunrise just increased the temperature by another few degrees. Very early one morning, the thermometer already showing eighty on the porch, I watched with such pleasure a few wisps of thin cloud obscuring the rising sun. But within an hour they had disappeared.

I took Judith to market where we met Miranda, Jonathan and Abie, who would take Judith back with them later that day. We all returned to Bel-Air where we found Hugh, Sally and Guy, just finishing the transformation of our jungle of a garden. In the broiling heat, they had apparently appeared out of the blue and, after spending time with Mike, had just got to work.

'We knew we wouldn't be able to cut it all back if you'd been here,' teased Hugh. I looked at my tidily clipped-back laurels and my weed-free terrace round the pool, the neatly cut lawns; and I forgave the few chopped down daisies, the little pink *guaria* that hadn't been noticed. Such kindness, in this intolerable heat and when they had so much to do at the golf course, was very moving. We rustled up a huge *salade niçoise* while they showered off the sweat and grass.

The next day I realised that there was something wrong with the pool pump. It was making a grating noise and the water was getting cloudy. We rang M. Escoffier who promised to come the following afternoon, which was Sunday. We had been invited to lunch by Ruth Thomas and I knew that, if I could persuade him to go, Mike would enjoy it. Delicious food and good company put him in a more relaxed mood, which was just as well, for M. Escoffier took one look at the pump, left and returned with a new one, costing over £300.

On Monday morning we were up early to go for a blood test. Dr Rouquié was jovial and reassuring. 'Well, at least it's you coming to see me, rather than the other way round,' he said to Mike. 'That has to be an improvement.'

After the surgery we shopped briefly and went home. Even this short excursion had worn him out. Raymond came by and they sat together on the porch. Then Jean appeared with two new friends, Andy and Maggie, who had recently bought a house not far away. We had seen the work on their house being carried out *en passant* and knew that Andy was a doctor and that they intended to live permanently in France on their retirement. We liked them at once and Raymond was very glad to meet them. Ordinarily Mike would have enjoyed holding court but he soon made his excuses and went to rest. I felt reassured to have a doctor not far away, even if he wasn't legally allowed to practise in France.

Later that afternoon Mike was anxious to make a booking for our return on the last motor-rail in the middle of September.

'I don't feel that I shall be well enough to drive home,' he said. He fretted until the booking was made and then seemed to relax. That night the heat was intense. There was not a breath of air. The next morning I opened all the doors and windows before seven but had to close them within an hour and by midday, the temperature in my house, with its metre-thick walls and all the shutters closed, was eighty-five degrees. In the afternoon, while Mike slept indoors. I took my chair and lay under my ash tree, depleted by the storm. The cows were lying down some three metres away. I covered my legs and arms with an anti-insect spray and fell asleep, my finger on the button. I woke to find the cows, the large mother cow in front, standing in a line close to the fence, all looking at me. They stayed immobile for several minutes before the mother nudged the others away for more cropping of the sparse, fast-yellowing grass. She remained alone, her large horns giving her a serious air, just sniffing me from a distance. Her great flanks quivered under the hordes of flies. I wondered if she could smell the insect spray. At last she moved away into the baking sunlight to join the others. The strong light on their backs, their muzzles away from the sun, patiently munching in a circle, they then inched back toward the shade from the tree, ears constantly flicking, now one, then the other, tails tossed languidly across their massive rumps.

The following day we had an appointment with the dermatologist in Villeneuve. We have air-conditioning in the car and when we parked and stepped outside, the town was like an oven. Dr Unanoe, a Basque, was very pleasant and read the notes from St George's Hospital without difficulty. He did not even examine Mike but I imagine that he could see that the blisters had gone. He seemed more concerned about reducing the steroids immediately and clearly thought that this should already have been done before we left London. 'Otherwise, Monsieur, your muscles will be badly affected,' he said. He then rang through to get the results of the blood test from Dr Rouquié and he looked grave. 'You have a slight kidney infection, you must continue with the antibiotics.' What else could go wrong? I thought. As we left Villeneuve I remarked on the smell of the drains, supposing it to be the result of the heat. However the smell seemed to persist and it was not until I reached home and opened the boot that I realised that I had carried a sack of rubbish, intended for the large *poubelle* in the village, all the way to Villeneuve and back. I was losing my grip.

Mike slept most of the rest of the day but in the evening announced his intention of going to the market in Monflanquin the following morning.

'I'll just sit in the square while you shop,' he said. He got up early, showered and shaved, and off we went. But he found it hard to even walk to a table and sit. I scurried round the stalls, we had a brief chat with the *ancien Maire,* and we came home. His temperature was up again. I called the doctor as instructed. '*Mais, le Docteur Rouquié est en vacances'*, said the secretary. Of course! It was the week of the medieval festival and in his other role as Deputy Mayor, Dr Rouquié was well known for the splendid costume in which he welcomed the arrival of Richard Coeur de Lion at the opening of the festivities. *La Doctoresse,* it was explained, had just finished her rounds and was about to eat. She would come as soon as she could. I sponged him down which made him shudder and Andy came and gave me moral support. When the doctor arrived she decided that the best solution was a few days in hospital on a drip. 'He'll soon be much better, you'll see,' she encouraged.

She began ringing round. Half an hour later she was still trying. There were three different medical teams who shared the Hospital St Cyr, in Villeneuve, we learnt, and none had a bed. We didn't realise then that we were just a small part of the crisis occurring in hospitals all over France due to the excessive heat coinciding with the annual holidays. Eventually she was advised that A&E would have a bed the following day if she could get him in now by ambulance. Another session of phone calls to find an ambulance. The eleventh one was successful. By this time, Raymond, Véronique, Jean, Hugh and Sally had all arrived and Mike was cheered as he was carried out across the parched grass into a luxurious ambulance. There was no room for me so Jean drove me to the hospital.

'Bring a book,' she said, with great forethought.

I felt completely unreal as we hurtled through the countryside. When we reached the hospital we found Mike, in his pyjamas, sitting in a small, but mercifully air conditioned, waiting room. He sat, without complaining, hands folded on his primitive walking stick, which he had cut in the wood years ago, and taken to using since he became so weak. We sat for four hours on hard metal chairs. We saw a young man whose ear had been gored by a cow, a little boy with a broken arm, a woman who carried a plastic bowl to vomit in; luckily she didn't need it.

Mike seemed calm and stoical, just longing to be in a bed under medical care. Jean and I read, which seemed to puzzle the other people waiting. I practically finished *The Master*, by C. P. Snow. I'm not sure if I would have bothered, in other circumstances. At midnight we saw the doctor. He was wisely not hurrying as he was the only one on duty with a long night before him. He was big, black and smiling, from Nouvelle Calédonie. By this time Mike had perked up. His fever had gone down a little. 'What's the matter with him?' queried the doctor. But when the results of a blood test came through within the hour, a kidney infection was confirmed and he was admitted. I handed all his medication over and Jean and I walked out into the hot, stifling night and came slowly home. It was almost three o'clock when she drove me up over the brow of the hill to Bel-Air. I was too exhausted to wonder if I would be nervous in the house on my own.

I awoke at seven and felt very wobbly. I had a shower and washed my hair. Raymond offered to drive me in at ten-thirty and we whirled along. Raymond was familiar with the hospital and we soon found Mike looking very cheerful in a spotless white gown, on a drip, in a lovely room with an en suite bathroom. There was one other bed but no one in it. I spoke to the Sister about his medication and everything seemed under control. He already looked so much better. We left at midday and Raymond offered to drive me in again later but Mike said that it wasn't necessary. He was clearly very content to be in safe hands and preferred to rest rather than make conversation. 'Not that I don't enjoy looking at you,' he said.

When I rang early that evening he told me that there was someone in the next bed who was very quiet. He said the nurses were super, and that he had enjoyed his lunch, which had consisted of soup, smoked salmon and prawns, grilled fish with courgettes and macaroni, green salad, cheese and dessert.

When I told Raymond, he laughed. '*C'est parce que c'est le quinze Août,*' he said. Of course! It was the feast of the Assumption. 'He won't be eating like that every day.'

It was a heavenly evening. I watered the hanging baskets, tested the pH in the pool. There was a gentle breeze, such a relief. And only 76 degrees on the porch. The sky was a hazy blue with puffs of white cloud shading to the faintest pink as the sun began to slide down. Jean-Michel's pigeons who had croo-crooed all afternoon on my roof had flown home to roost. I looked through the open door, and straight through the house. Out of the window, framed in creeper, I could see the tops of the maize caught in the evening light, and the grey, purple haze of the hills on the far side of the river Lot. A small green tree frog plopped onto the leg of the table, clambered up slowly through the umbrella hole, paused for a moment then took off again, landing on my hand. There he just sat, being cool. I waited until he jumped off again and went to bed.

CHAPTER SEVENTEEN

The next morning I phoned at eight-thirty. A faint voice answered but I could not make out what he said and, thinking that it must be the quiet stranger in the next bed, I apologised and rang off. Within five minutes my phone rang. It was the doctor. She said something that I did not understand then added, 'Your husband cannot speak. He needs you, Madame. Please drive carefully.'

I stood, shaking, then rang Raymond who told me on no account to drive myself. He raced Jean and me along the winding road to the hospital. At one point in the twenty-minute drive he was so frantic I had to calm him.

We knew now that Mike had had a stroke and found him at last, in a different, single room on the second floor, flushed and dreadfully restless. He had difficulty breathing and I thought he was going to die within the hour. I just wanted to reassure him somehow and sat, holding his hand, talking, almost willing him to die peacefully. I couldn't bear that he should have to suffer anymore. Gradually he grew calmer.

The young doctor whom we called Doctor Blue Eyes did her rounds. We never could remember her name but her astonishingly beautiful eyes were intelligent and sympathetic.

'If he survives today there is hope,' she said. We sent Raymond home. By the evening Mike's breathing had improved. He knew us. We had established one squeeze of the hand for yes, two for no. That evening I was told very firmly to go home and rest. Our new friends, Maggie and Doctor Andy brought up a basket containing the most delicious meal for Jean and me. They had guests and wisely knew that we would be too exhausted to want to eat with others and make conversation. We were both surprised to find that we were ravenous.

The next morning while I sat by his bed, my two sons walked into the room. It was like the cavalry arriving. Hugh and Sally came later, Claudette and Raymond during the afternoon and Jean; and so began a routine of arriving at ten and leaving at eight-thirty. I sang to him a lot, quietly, especially before leaving him, as much to keep up my own spirits as for him.

We took short breaks for food when others took over our vigil. We were entitled to a ticket for a subsidised meal in the hospital canteen but the food was pretty basic and we preferred to go out into Villeneuve. Just spending twenty minutes away from the hospital in a world where people went about their normal business of the day was a relief.

The nursing was very efficient. At first it was difficult to distinguish the nurses from other staff as they all wore spotless white. Gradually faces became familiar. Mike's bed linen and chemise were changed every day, and twice if necessary. He had always already been washed and shaved when I arrived. There were two senior nurses, one optimist, the other not. Miss Pessimist, as we dubbed her, took us aside after the third day and said that Mike was unlikely to ever speak again or even to regain enough movement to be accepted in a rehabilitation centre. We all cried. Putney Home and Hospital for Incurables, euthanasia, we thought about it all.

Hugh and Sally, with Guy, were the optimistic brigade. They brought pencils and a drawing block. Although it was his left side that was paralysed, the right hand, once so skilled at drawing, careered all over the page. But we did have some success and he greeted me the following day with a very slurred 'How's the pool?' He began to massage his left arm and do face exercises. Sometimes he spoke, seldom coherently, at others he just slept. Daily physiotherapy began after he had been hauled out of bed with a hoist and tied in a chair for an hour.

'I want to go home,' he said very clearly and grumpily one morning. The next day there was no response at all. Adam had looked up information on the Net and learnt that stroke patients often made strides at three-day intervals, the other two days being just recuperation.

While he slept we did crosswords to pass the time. At one point Matthew said, 'I don't actually know what 'salacious' means.' A voice from the bed said croakily, but clearly, 'Dirty-minded.'

'No, Dad,' replied Adam, airily. 'That won't do. It's something R, something R, something, something, something.'

There was the briefest of pauses. 'Prurient,' said Mike.

We treated ourselves to a meal at the Vietnamese restaurant that evening to celebrate. We finished with liqueurs, which when drained revealed, I was told, very rude marbles in the bottom. They were lost on me, as I couldn't see them without my glasses.

We were instructed to sit on Mike's paralysed side to stimulate the damaged side of his brain. He was propped up as there was a danger of the chest infection returning. He had lost so much weight that his ring kept slipping off and he gave it to me for safekeeping.

When we got home that night, I swam to relax my tired muscles. I awoke at two o'clock and realised that the ring was no longer on my finger. In a panic I got up, put on the pool light and ran out into the garden. It must have come off in the water. Could it have gone into the skimmers? I had no idea. How could I have been so careless? The ring was one of a pair with my wedding ring, and had been specially designed for us by a friend, so many years ago. It seemed a terribly bad omen. But as I ran up the steps, something glinted in the moonlight. There, by the side of the pool where I had dried myself, lay the small thick, decorated band of gold, which matched my own. I picked it up and slid it onto the chain round my neck. I sat outside in the moonlight, until, in spite of the warmth of the night, I began to shiver.

Adam had to leave after a few days but promised to return at the weekend with reinforcements. He and Caz had already booked for their annual holiday at Bel-Air and Elliot and Thomas badly wanted to come. Until they arrived, Matthew, who was officially on holiday from working on *Bombay Dreams* and could stay, took turns with me at Mike's bedside, and other friends and neighbours gave us constant support. We returned to Bel-Air one evening to find the most beautifully arranged vase of sunflowers outside the door. Ruth Thomas arrived with a radio for Mike and the cousins who lived in Villeneuve offered us a bed, anytime. But strangely, as I became used to it, the drive home at the end of the day was quite soothing, after so many hours of anxious inactivity while Mike slept. Fields of sunflowers were already turning colour, their heavy heads bending over. The road was especially beautiful where it curved between two great expanses of maize. On one side the soft, fluffy, pale green duvet of flowers of the edible variety; on the other, that for cattle feed, the rows more rigidly defined with spiky, pinkish red flowers.

Matthew and I cleared out the boys' room and made the beds. I wondered how they would cope with their sick grandpa. While we existed in a small world between home and hospital, village life went on. There was a grand wedding at the big house. As the family were Protestant the ceremony was to take place in the Temple in Monflanquin and Raymond was engaged to chauffeur the bride in the old car, suitably decorated. He had to buy new trousers. *'Farce qu'il a trop mangé,'* teased Claudette. 'It's not true,' grunted Raymond, then he shrugged and smiled.

It was market day at Villeneuve, and Miranda and Jonathan left Abie with friends and came to see Mike. He smiled at Miranda looking so beautiful in her long orange dress. We saw another doctor, newly returned from holiday. He was pleased with Mike's progress but worried about signs of atrial fibulation. I explained that this was an old problem, which he had developed many years before when he was trying to combine occasional commuting to teach in an American university with working on BBC children's television, while also teaching at Goldsmiths.

'We would like to give him an anticoagulant,' said the doctor. 'But it could make the bruise in his brain spread, so we can't risk it.' He sighed. '*Courage, Madame.*'

Hugh and Sally arrived at lunchtime and banished us from the sickroom to go and eat. The pavement cafés were crowded. The waiter, recognising us, squeezed us in, but when Jonathan ordered cheese with his *omelette aux cèpes* his eyebrows almost disappeared. '*Sacrilège!*' he declared.

It rained hard in the night but the temperature did not fall. With the air so moist it felt more like the Caribbean. Raymond and Claudette came in to see Mike, with Jean-Michel and Véronique. They also had another patient in the hospital to visit as the young man who usually drives the combine had slipped while vaulting over an electric fence. Unwisely he had grabbed the live *piquet,* which gave him a shock and caused him to fall so awkwardly that he had broken his femur. Mike seemed very sleepy and it was difficult to rouse him. '*Ouvrez les yeux,* Michel!' yelled the nurses each time they came along. He would make an effort but not for long. We drove home hoping that the grandchildren would get a better result the next day.

Jean had taken the day off to cook a huge lasagne and she brought it up just before they arrived. The boys tumbled out of the car, which I was surprised to see was chauffeur driven. The TGV had arrived on time in Agen but the office for the already booked and paid for hire car was shut. Adam learnt, next day, that the car keys had been left with the man who runs the station buffet. As there was no way he could possibly have known of this cavalier arrangement and as the taxi had cost eighty pounds he was not best pleased. The hire car arrived in Villeneuve the next morning and he did, eventually, get his taxi fare refunded.

Now we were a complete family and Matthew was able to take the odd morning off. He had been such a strong support but the constant anxiety was beginning to take its toll. He and Thomas swam. Elliot too, swallowing a lot of water as he chirped away with an endless recital of interesting information. The whole world fascinates him. Long may it last. Claudette appeared with melons, and an egg loaf. She had obviously got the idea from the *pain poisson* we had eaten at the tenth wedding anniversary. This one was made with ten eggs mixed with small pieces of courgette, carrot, onion and lardons and cooked for forty-five minutes in a very slow oven. 'In a *bain-marie?*' I asked. '*Non,*' she replied, simply. It was delicious.

We established a visiting rota, which gave all of us

a little time off. On August the 27th Caz and I did the late shift and Mike was more animated. As I adjusted his pillow he looked at me with his eyes wide open.

'It's a big stroke,' he said, refuting what I had told him at the beginning. The physiotherapist had been again and was pleased with the improvement in his movement on the paralysed side. 'He is really trying hard,' he said. Only his chest was still causing concern. I sat listening hour after hour to the hiss of the oxygen and wondering how soon we could get him home. Adam had been in touch with our GP who promised to do her best with the stroke unit at St George's. As I drove back later to Bel-Air with my daughter-in-law on another beautiful evening, I compared the drive with that from Clapham to Tooting and tried to count my blessings. When we got home we found a barbecue prepared for Matthew's birthday. We ate the last of the *pain aux oeufs* for a starter. It was even better after three days.

The next day, after a long session with the hospital administrator, we began to make plans to fly Mike home as soon as the doctor would release him. Clearly his recovery was going to be a slow and lengthy process and we had already run up a sizeable bill, only part of which would be covered by the E111. We had already established that our travel insurance would cover neither this, nor an air ambulance. The insurance company had contacted our GP and it was clear that Mike had forgotten to add to his form the latest medication for the angina. I sat, for my twenty minutes off duty, by the fountain in the garden of the hospital, great cedar trees bordering the shady lawns. I thought how unimportant the money was. We were fortunate to have some savings. What else were savings for?

It was almost the end of August and, although it was still summer heat, the leaves were turning. Jean, who had been such a wonderful support, had closed her studio and her little house and left for England, and Maggie and Andy had to leave later that day. We know how hard it is to go when the weather is so beautiful. We continued with our daily vigil. We drove into the hospital every morning, past the unusual and somehow curiously reassuring statue of the mother lion and her three cubs at the wide entrance. We now took a short cut up to Mike's room. There was a door in the corridor which said FUNERARIUM. We had made grim jokes about it when we first passed it. Now one of the nurses had shown us that if we pushed open this door and walked up the back staircase, it opened almost opposite his door. The boys came for a brief visit every other day. Elliot chatted but Thomas found it hard. Every so often we were gently expelled from the room while some procedure was carried out. Doctor Blue Eyes showed me the results of a chest X-ray. They did not look good. The nurses came yet again to aspirate his chest. His breathing was laboured. I sat in his room hour after hour just willing the new and stronger antibiotic to do its work. But he looked so tired and frail, as though he was just too exhausted to battle on. And still I hoped.

On the last day of August, Caz and I stayed for the evening session. His breathing was much better but for the first time for weeks there was a little breeze outside and his hands seemed cold. I closed the door onto the small balcony and lowered the blinds. Before I left I asked the nurse for a blanket, kissed him and gently covered him. Did they know? I'm not sure. Had they hinted, I would have stayed. But they didn't and I left, as usual. The next morning, before eight o'clock, they rang me to say that my husband had just died peacefully in his sleep.

Matthew, Adam and I walked up the stairs for the last time. Mike lay, so thin, under the snowy sheet, like an effigy. They had propped up his chin with a folded cloth, but too high. It made the corners of his generous mouth turn down as if he thoroughly disapproved of dying. We kissed him and tried to comprehend the incomprehensible. One of the staff came in and asked if I had brought his clothes. It had never occurred to me to do so. His clean pyjamas were in the cupboard, which he had never worn since his stroke.

Would these do? She shrugged. We were asked to leave. He would be moved – downstairs. They were sympathetic but for them it was routine. We should go and see the administrator.

We seemed to spend the next few hours wandering from one office to another, cancelling arrangements for the air ambulance, filling in endless forms and paying bills. The hospital phoned the funeral director. We had an appointment for the following morning. They would need Mike's parents' Christian names and his mother's maiden name. Still in a daze, we called in at the farm on our way home. I couldn't cry at all but they were both in tears.

'Oh, *pauvre Michel,*' sobbed Claudette. 'And no more of those wonderful trips we all made together on a Sunday.' Until then I hadn't realised just how much they had meant to her.

That evening Colin Slee, the Dean of Southwark Cathedral, phoned for news and was very sad. He told me that Edith and Rachel, his wife and daughter, were somewhere in France. The next day, M. Guyou, my neighbour, who in 25 years had never come to my door, came to shake my hand. He made the excuse that one of his cows was out. He told me that a woman aged 61 had dropped dead two days before at the fête in the next village. They had given her *bouche-à-bouche,* he said, but to no avail. I wasn't sure if this news was supposed to cheer me in some way, but he shook my hand again, wiped away a tear and left. Half an hour later I had a call from Edith Slee. She and Rachel were some three hours drive away. They would be with us by four o'clock. When I protested she said, 'Stop arguing, I just want to give you a hug.'

I needed a hug after a session with the undertaker.

The whole process seemed macabre. Getting Mike's body back to England was not a simple affair. Elaborate coffins are the norm as cremations are uncommon and, as we strove for something simple and less tasteless, the young woman, surrounded by wreaths and urns and pieces of marble, looked disappointed. Did we want a coffin with a window in it? They had many Italian customers who apparently insisted on it. Mafia and substitute bodies came inevitably to mind. The documents would have to be signed by the *Préfecture*. It would take time. She would have to liaise with a funeral director in London.

We came out into the sunlight in a sort of trance and walked back again to the hospital to settle yet another bill. Did we want to go down the staircase this time and into the *Funerarium* where Mike's body lay? I could see that this was going to be very difficult for both my sons and so we decided not to. Raymond and Claudette went that afternoon and now I wish I had gone with them. But we went back to Bel-Air and sat in the garden until Edith and Rachel arrived with a candle. We lit it for Mike.

The next candles which were lit for him were those

in the cathedral where his body lay the night before his wonderful funeral two weeks later. Mike joined the army at the age of eighteen and vowed that he would never join anything ever again. He never did. The one exception he made was to become a proud member of the Guild of Stewards at Southwark, the most forward-looking, loving and inclusive cathedral in London.

CHAPTER EIGHTEEN

'Will you go back to Bel-Air?' people asked me.

'Of course,' I replied.

'Won't you find it difficult?'

'I imagine so.'

How would I feel? I knew that many in my situation who had tried, had found it impossible. A second home is such an intensely shared adventure. A madcap decision in the first place but, for Mike and me, it had given us more than 25 years of special summers together and these memories remain to be cherished. Bel-Air is very important to me and I am blessed.

On Easter Monday all the family, except Matthew, who had to work, flew Ryanair to Bergerac. The flight was fine; I cannot recommend the sandwiches. From the modern mammoth which is now Stansted, it is the first time I have ever travelled to Bergerac; back, it seemed, almost to the time of Biggles, with cars parked casually on the grass and a small tent for the swift and efficient baggage-handling. Within fifteen minutes of landing we were on the road in a substantial hired car. Already the right side of Bergerac for us, we soon took a left turn to Issegeac, coasted round the outskirts of Villereal, another thirteen-century *bastide* with a wonderful covered market square and, in less than an hour, Monflanquin was clearly visible at the end of about the only straight stretch of road in Lot-et-Garonne.

Bel-Air was waiting for us, clean and sparkling, thanks to Susan. On the table outside stood a large pot planted with daffodils bearing a note of welcome from Ursula. Claudette had opened the shutters and laid the fire, and a jug of tulips and forsythia from her garden lit up the living room. I stood in the doorway looking up towards the wood. A breeze blew down across the vineyard. The cows were grazing quietly. I was home.

The boys piled out of the car and rushed into the chilly house. They quickly got warm as they struggled to carry out all the odd pieces of garden furniture, which had been stored in their room during the winter. We filled the hot water bottles, lit a blazing fire, and soon all the sheets and pillows were aired. Fortunately Bel-Air is not a damp house. Unaccustomed to an almost full house this early in the year, I was short of bedding and I had arranged with Jean to borrow duvets for the boys. She would arrive in her snug little village house in two days' time and her neighbour Rosaleen would have already switched on her central heating. Bel-Air has no such luxury and I had forewarned Elliot and Thomas that they would find it a very different experience from high summer. April can be unpredictable with frosty nights and, once we were no longer subject to school holidays, Mike and I usually left our spring visit until May. Jean's house is very attractive, with much of her work on the walls. I would be glad to see her. We gathered up the duvets and posted Jean's key through Rosaleen's letter box. The beds all made, we put a guard around the fire at Bel-Air, the living room already beginning to warm up, and went down to the farm where Claudette had already invited us for supper. Once again we passed what looked like two newly constructed houses at the bottom of our track. No doubt we would soon find out to whom they belonged.

Raymond and Claudette were waiting to greet us. All too conscious that one of us was missing, we sadly rearranged our traditional seating round the table. But, unused to eating indoors here, the boys were unaware, and this helped. Also, Clement, Raymond's grandson, was staying that week and came to give the customary kisses all round. The boys eyed each other. It would probably be another year before they would feel confident enough to try out their tentative English and French – at least in front of the adults. As we ladled out the soup, Raymond talked about the new houses. 'Are they local people?' I asked. He hesitated. *'Ils ne sont pas exactement du coin,'* he said.

I imagined folk from Agen perhaps, or even Bergerac. But it transpired that one of the new occupants was a butcher from Monflanquin, the other house owned by a relation of the farmer about two kilometres away. Clearly our *coin* was, as far as Raymond was concerned, very small indeed. I was pleased to have permanent residents at the bottom of our track as it makes an opportunist burglar less likely. The houses had been built on a piece of land at the end of which stood a complete ruin. There was just one back wall, a heap of stones, and curiously, still standing near the road, a solitary stone gatepost. It had always amused me, for on the top was a neatly cemented pot of flourishing house leeks. This long-abandoned ruin was the reason that building permission for the new houses had been granted, a house having once been there.

'But why didn't they demolish the ruin and use the stones?' I asked, as I had noticed that it was still there, quite close and at a very odd angle to the furthest house.

'That would have been too expensive,' explained Raymond as Claudette carried in the first asparagus of the season. 'Perhaps they'll use them later to build a wall.'

Thomas enjoyed the whole meal, which continued with cabbage stuffed with minced pork, galantine of chicken, and a copious salad of endive. Claudette grows the endive, which I love, in enamel buckets in the darkest part of the *cave*. Elliot, who is a difficult eater, enjoyed his customary bread dipped in a bowl of olive oil, but rejoined the menu for a very large sponge cake filled with *crème anglaise,* with which we drank the first of the season's white wine which they still make themselves.

I thanked Raymond for having organised someone to cut back my pampas grass. I hadn't had much of a chance to inspect it but I could see that the normally tall and shaggy, sprawling clumps at the far end of the pool had been reduced to strange, rounded, humped figures. From a distance they looked like great, crouching, bald bears. The work had been done by the mysterious Bernard, of whom I had heard but never met. It was Ken Farrington, our English neighbour, who had discovered Bernard. He was apparently a good all-round handy man who would tackle anything and charged, very reasonably, by the hour. In the summer he lived with a group of friends in a nearby village but during the winter he stayed at Ken's house and kept an eye on things while carrying out minor repairs. I looked forward to meeting him. We also learnt that

M. Carpentier had had a serious accident with a hose of liquid cement which had become blocked and then suddenly spurted out damaging one of his eyes. *'Il est vraiment demoralisé,'* said Raymond.

Elliot, who had just started piano lessons, was persuaded to play one of his first pieces and then Clement surprised us all with a short recital. On several occasions he had come shyly to listen when I played. When I showed him how to find the melody of *Au Clair de la Lune,* he had learnt it in seconds. He had been having lessons for six months now, he told us, and clearly he has inherited the musical gene in Claudette's side of the family. Elliot was impressed.

As we left, with a dozen eggs and a small electric radiator, we admired the new heavy sliding glass doors enclosing the hangar. Jean-Michel's plastic screens had finally fallen to pieces, they explained. The room now looked so smart, I thought, there would be no chance of our ever returning the space to *'non habitable'.* The great lemon tree in its tub on wheels was hung with fruit, and together with all the other sun-loving plants huddled along one wall, still awaited warmer weather. The air was chilly, the sky bright with stars. We were all tired. As I lay in bed that first night, wondering if I would sleep, the house put its arms around me and the next thing I knew was the call of Jean-Michel's hens as daylight filtered through the window. I got up quietly and found the small bellows. The still hot ashes soon glowed and then a small flame licked the kindling and rose through the dry sticks to light the fire for a new day.

Later, while Adam shopped, I went to the bank. The Credit Agricole was completely transformed. Where once we would wait in conversational lines amid the potted plants, wondering if we had picked the slowest queue yet again, where talk was of prunes and maize and cows and Brussels, of celebratory meals and new babies; all was now space and silence. The counter was gone where fresh-faced young men, it was usually men, in smart jackets in deep emerald green or bright blue would smile and chat as they tapped with beautifully manicured fingers into their small computers. Now, around the newly curved, bare wall, four machines apparently coped with everything. At a tiny desk in the centre perched Miss Chewing-Gum. We called her that when, some two years ago, she first joined the young men. With her pale skin, heavy eyelids and full greased lips in perpetual motion we were surprised that no one checked this mesmerising habit which gave her such a, probably false, air of insolence. In her new role as receptionist and the only human being in sight, it seemed that she had been told. She chewed no longer. A slight waft of sympathy came my way as I explained why I wished to change my house insurance into my name. For the first time, Mike's original death certificate in French did not need translation. I waited while she telephoned, some distance it seemed, for instructions.

'*Oui. C'est Monflanquin,*' she repeated. Eventually there were endless forms to be signed in triplicate. Having still not completed all the paperwork in London, my probate forms having been lost during the postal strike, these I found doubly distressing. I'm not sure why. At last it seemed all was finished. When I then asked her which machine I should use to put some English money into my account she looked worried. More phonecalls followed. At last she unwound her long legs, slid off her stool and ushered me across the quiet, carpeted space to a solid door in the corner and knocked. I was admitted to a tiny booth where a solitary woman, completely enclosed behind plate glass, told me to post my notes through a small slit high up in the window. Not for her the usual friendly contact with customers. At no time was I shaken by the hand or invited to sit down. It was all very un-French and dispiriting.

We went up into Monflanquin hoping to drink coffee in the sunshine. Two of the restaurants had not yet opened for the season. The other, never very accommodating, declined to serve us anything except a meal. There were changes, too, going on in the square and down the two steeply sloping streets.

New pavements were being laid, a large cement mixer ground incessantly and there was a great deal of noise and dust. We thought that coffee at home would be cheaper and certainly quieter.

It was a beautiful day and after lunch outside we decide to tackle the garden. The quiet was shattered as the strimmer whined away, Adam following me with the lawnmower. I was sad as, inevitably, swathes of buttercups, grape hyacinths, coltsfoot and marguerites fell beneath the blades. The boys did a minimum of raking before they discovered the *boules* and were soon arguing and laughing and looking for the tape measure. Bernard had put all the cuttings from the pampas grass on the edge of the field and when Raymond came by on the tractor he said we could burn it the following morning if there was not too much wind. We cooked pork chops on a griddle over the fire that night and Hugh and Sally called unexpectedly to invite us all to eat with them on Friday. Later we made up the fire again. It fascinated the boys, especially when we piled on dry fir cones, which soon glowed like a miniature forest of scarlet. Without television we played charades, Scrabble, cards and wink murder, something new to me. This can be played as an adjunct to any another game. Lots are drawn and the aim of the murderer is not to be discovered as the players keel over after receiving a discreet wink. Elliot's winking was so unsubtle we were all hysterical. By eleven p.m. it was the adults who were tired.

We spent the next morning making a huge bonfire with the heap of cut pampas grass on the field. The boys were really captivated as the fire licked and blazed and, as the wind gusted, they were chased by heat and smoke. In their world of electronic delights this primitive force was exciting. They wielded barrows, forks and rakes and we burnt every bit of rubbish we could find while Caz and Adam worked in tandem with mower and strimmer. After lunch I unearthed the pump for the weedkiller and, having worked out how to use it, set to all down the drive, which now looked as though it had never seen a load of stones two years ago. Apart from grass it was green with clover and edged with buttercups, dandelions, speedwell, and honesty. I tried to avoid the honesty.

On market day the sun shone. We bowled along, dazzled by the fields of rape on either side of the road.

The market was crowded. People stopped every few yards to greet each other between the stalls, more numerous than usual because of the Easter holiday. There were small lemon trees and heaps of fat, glistening *pruneaux*. There were boxes of early, but really ripe, strawberries, small and irregular, marked *'Fraises déformées. 2'éme choix'*. At 2.50 Euros for 500

wind had displaced. He would fix them. He talked about working as a stone mason on the Château of Biron some years ago. He was gentle and honest and before we left I gave him a key to the *chai* and instructions to fix the roof and just cut the grass now and then. Another problem solved.

On Saturday we invited Raymond and Claudette and Jean to eat at the new restaurant Le Chabrol, at St Aubin. In our region, no wine is drunk before the soup and to *faire chabrol,* is to pour the first wine into the still warm soup bowl, wiped clean with bread, and drink it from there. A new restaurant only ten minutes away! We were eager to try it. There had been talk of one opening in our village but it had come to nought. Even the shop was still trying to find someone to take it on. Raymond had assured us that the food at this new venue was good.

'*Oui, la cuisine est bonne,*' he confirmed. '*Mais...*' he pulled a face. He had eaten there with a reunion of the *Crédit Agricole,* he explained, and the service had been so slow that the meal had taken well over three hours, but this was probably an exception. We arrived, however, just in time to see a convoy of cars disgorging a local *Club de Pétanque.*

'*Merde,*' said Raymond. 'We'd better get our orders in first.'

The restaurant was already almost full. The *pétanque* players, some thirty of them by now, were to be accommodated in a further room at a slightly lower level. We ordered aperitifs and got down to the menu with unusual speed. There were three to choose from. The first at 13 Euros, about £8.50, was a choice between soup or salad, followed by beef with shallots and three vegetables, or *navarin* of lamb. To finish there was a cheese and walnut salad, *crème brulee* or two *boules* of ice cream.

The most expensive menu at exactly double the price, offered, as a starter, *Marmite de la mer en croûte*, or *salade gourmande* with *foie gras*, *magret de canard fumé* and asparagus. This was followed either by crown of lamb with rosemary, duck breast cut into a fan shape, or an *entrecôte façon Rossini*, all served with *tomates provençales*, *frites maison*, and *endives braisées*. The dessert was a choice between a small goat's cheese warmed with honey, strawberry tart or ice cream.

We all decided that the middle menu at 18 Euros looked good and settled down to choose between three starters consisting of a salad with goats cheese, semi-cooked *foie gras*, or *sandre*, a river fish, with tiny vegetables in a puff pastry case. The main course was either *confit de canard*, or an entrecôte served with a Roquefort sauce, shallots, or sea salt.

The first course was quickly served and delicious. I had the fish and it was sufficiently generous a portion to make the predicted long wait for my steak bearable.

We watched the family of twelve at the next table while Raymond, pronouncing his *foie gras* very good, gave a *sotto voce* running commentary. He explained who was married to whom. The family ranged from a baby asleep in the pram and a peripatetic toddler, to the great uncle of 93. A retired priest, according to Raymond, he sat at the head of the table, his beret still on his head and clearly enjoyed his food. From time to time his eyes closed for about ten minutes. The family appeared not to notice. An occasional round of cheering from the *pétanque* players in the other room would wake him, after which he would brighten up again and take charge of the conversation.

While we waited, Raymond told us about being waylaid in Monflanquin the previous week by a reporter for a local television station who was researching the mysterious goings on of the family at the nearby Chateau of Martel. I was interested as it was Mme Marchand, the daughter of the family who, with her husband Jean, had been responsible for the past seventeen years for the wonderful music festival in Monflanquin. The sudden demise of this popular event two years previously had shocked and disappointed everyone and, apart from rumours, no one really knew the reason.

'*C'était quelque chose bizarre, une grande famille comme ça*' said Raymond shaking his head. 'I told the fellow I didn't want to discuss it.'

According to an article in the local paper, it seemed that Mme Marchand had been completely taken in by a confidence trickster in Paris, Raymond continued. Having estranged her from her husband he had slowly taken over the finances of the entire family. 'I'll show you the report,' said Raymond. *'C'était vraiment incroyable,'* he said mournfully. He cheered up when his steak arrived, barely cooked, as he likes it. He told me that the restaurant, now completely full and buzzing, the *pétanque* players especially animated, used to be the *boulangerie* when he was a boy. It was here he came during the war to get the bread.

'They had no bread in Paris,' he said, 'but here there was always a bit of wheat somewhere.' He smiled, tapping his nose. 'You know, *sous la table.'* He was looking forward to an outing the following morning with *le Club des Vieilles Voitures* but the weather forecast was not good.

Sunday dawned very damp and grey and there were frequent electricity cuts. After lunch it brightened and the rest of my family set off on an expedition to the medieval Château of Bonaguil. Claudette, pleased that she had not accompanied Raymond – it had actually been raining when he left – came to visit me bringing the newspaper article. Written after an interview with M. Marchand and his son-in-law, the story was indeed bizarre. Apparently, a few days after the end of the last music festival, M. Marchand had been confronted by his wife and her two brothers – one of whom was a doctor in Bordeaux – and had been accused of having 45 mistresses. Jean Marchand is a slightly built, very calm and quiet man. I would never have imagined him able to cope with two or three mistresses, let alone 45. He was given half an hour to pack and was put on a train for Paris, since when, all communication with his wife and family had ceased. Next his newly married daughter suddenly left her husband, selling all her shares and returning to the Château. The mystery man, named only as M. Thierry T., had apparently gained complete domination over Mme Marchand, claiming to be working, it was said, for the Secret Service, and protecting the family against Freemasons. M. Thierry T., however, was already associated with fraud and with several organisations which had ended up in liquidation.

'But how did she get so taken in?' I asked. Mme Marchand had always seemed to me intelligent and businesslike.

Claudette shrugged. *'C'était vraiment impensable,'* she said. The story continued with the doctor closing his practice in Bordeaux, and returning to the Château. His wife, who, apparently, hated country life, stopped phoning her friends and sold her smart apartment near Arcachon, which she adored. When her nephew asked the *notaire,* to whom the cheque from the sale was made out, it was to M. Thierry T. A reporter had at one time been courteously received at the Château by one of the younger grandchildren who had sadly but firmly declared it to be a private affair. More recently the bailiffs had been sent in and the furniture removed, no taxes having been paid for several years. Now, the Château was empty.

'But where are they living?' I asked. Claudette did not know. 'Everyone is baffled,' she said. It seemed such a sad end for a family. I remembered especially the grandmother who, although 91 and lame, had always welcomed everyone so graciously to the lovely garden of the Château on those magical summer evenings of such wonderful music.

After Claudette had gone I sat alone for the first time. It was very peaceful in the early evening sunlight. I had been right to come and knew now that I would return in the summer. I thought of all the joy that Bel-Air has embraced within its thick walls but also all the sorrow. Anaïs's father-in-law, Pierre, born in 1839, was married at 27, and a widower at 40, with three little boys to care for. Anaïs herself was just 48 when her husband Justin died of a heart attack and she had only her handicapped son to help her make a frugal living from the land. She lived to be 92 and *vaillante,* valiant, is the word those who knew her use to describe her.

She sets a good example.

She kept her school reading books and marked the passages which she clearly reread, especially in her small and worn copy of *La petite Jeanne,* which gives advice on everything from crops to hygiene to widowhood. I had recently been rereading another of her books, *Le Tour de France par deux Enfants,* which is the cleverest geography book. I got it down again from the shelf. This exciting tale of two orphans, escaping from occupied France after the annexing of Alsace-Lorraine and journeying the length of the country to find their uncle must have enthralled generations of pupils. There are 212 engravings showing every region of France and what went on there in 1884 when this, the 128th edition, was printed. Anaïs's copy being somewhat tattered, Simone bought me the latest edition, number 8566 *mille,* and there is an updated Prologue of 1904 telling proudly of the wonderful inventions of X-ray, chloroform, submarines, photography, the telephone, the first Metro. It is, of course, full of moral precepts. They fall oddly on the modern ear. But this little, old fashioned book, full of national pride, is strangely moving.

'Si, partout en France, même dans le moindre coin, chacun veut remplir son devoir, la patrie deviendra grande, heureuse, prospère. Que les plus courageux donnent l'exemple, les autres suivront. L'exemple est contagieux, tâchons qu'il soit toujours bon.'

'If, in the whole of France, even in the smallest corner, everyone will fulfil their duties, our country will become great, happy and prosperous. When the most courageous set the example, others will follow. An example is contagious, take care that the one you set is good.'

No one reads moral tales now, but I am told that *citoyenneté* is now on the agenda once more in French schools and must be somehow included in every lesson. Once a year, at the end of September, Monflanquin celebrates *La soirée du Patrimoine*. The crowd, mostly local, winds up the narrow medieval streets, which are lit with small candles on ledges. Costumed figures from literature and the history of the town recite from balconied windows. Children gaze in wonder as they listen to poems by Ronsard, tales of the Black Prince, and of the Huguenots. They hear of the founding of the town and the rights and responsibilities set down in the original charter in 1256. There is a real sense of history here. Bel-Air is not visible from Monflanquin, but the curiously shaped hill under which it nestles is clear. Orchards and vineyards, woods and hedges can all disappear but this gentle landscape remains.

From my porch I can see up to the wood, where each day the trees grow greener against the dark conifers. The vines, like rows of withered arms against the stakes, give no hint as yet of the luxury of foliage and fruit to come. There is a blaze of kerria against the barn wall and the fig is just beginning to leaf, the tiny first crop already showing beneath the buds. This morning the cuckoo was calling. Every summer we escaped the city and came here. We enjoyed our friends, those who live here and those who came to spend time with us. At Bel-Air, somehow, everything was renewed; our health and strength, our peace of mind, our sense of what was important, and our love. The house was, is, a special place. I shall come as often and for as long as I am able. The next generation, and the one after that will, I hope and trust, continue to find here, as Mike and I have done, something of lasting value in their busy lives.

ACKNOWLEDGEMENTS

Thanks to Tony and Nan White

A HOUSE IN THE SUNFLOWERS

BY RUTH SILVESTRE

This is the story of a dream come true. In 1976, in the Lot-et-Garonne region of south-west France, Ruth Silvestre and her family found Bel-Air de Grèzelongue, a house that had been left, deserted and uninhabited, for ten years. They fell in love with it.

A House in the Sunflowers tells of their affair with the house, from the search and initial frustrations, their euphoria when they finally bought it and the challenges of renovation and gradual assimilation into the local community. It provides rare glimpses of French family life in the region that is considered the gastronomic centre of France, complete with mouth-watering descriptions of meals in the sun and fascinating insights into the history and customs of this area.

A HARVEST OF SUNFLOWERS

BY RUTH SILVESTRE

Twenty years after first setting eyes on Bel-Air de Grèzelongue, her dream house in the sunflowers in south-west France, Ruth Silvestre brings us the long-awaited sequel to the adventures.

Local friendships and bonds of loyalty that she and her family formed during the gradual restoration of their once derelict farmhouse have now deepened. The children, both hers and her neighbours, are now adults. Wedding festivities and banquets are described in mouth-watering detail as, with natural *joie-de-vivre*, a close-knit society celebrates and prepares for the coming generation.

A Harvest of Sunflowers is a joy to read from a writer who can illustrate the simplest experience with exuberance and affection. Both moving and highly amusing, this book will hold the reader.